SIGNS AND SYMBOLS IN EDUCATION

EDUCATIONAL SEMIOTICS

François Victor Tochon, Ph.D.
University of Wisconsin-Madison, USA

Blue Mounds, Wisconsin

Deep Institute Online !
For updates and more resources
Visit the Deep Institute Website:
deepinstitute.org

Copyright © 2013 by Poiesis Creations Ltd - *Deep Education Press*
Member of Independent Book Publishers Association (IBPA)

All rights reserved. Permission is granted to copy or reprint portions up to 5% of the book for noncommercial use, except they may not be posted online without written permission from the publisher.
For permissions, contact: publisher@deepeducationpress.org

ISBN   978-1-939755-01-8 (pb)
        978-1-939755-27-8 (hb)
        978-1-939755-14-8 (eBook)

Library of Congress Cataloging-in-Publication Data
1. Semiotics. 2. Second Language Acquisition—Study and teaching.
3. Communication. 4. Tochon, Francois Victor

Keywords: Educational Signs and Symbols – Semiotics – Research Methods – Teacher Education – Student Teaching – Education

Target audience: Collegiate semiotics instructors – education instructors – second language acquisition – semiotics and media studies researchers – media studies and cultural studies students – teacher educators – graduate students - university researchers

Topics: semiotics, applied semiotics, e-portfolios, teacher education, world languages, preservice teacher, narrative analysis, actantial analysis, pedagogy, authenticity, curriculum, semiotics, genre, premises, situation models, indexation, oral communication

Version 1
Proofreading: Nathan J. Black, Kristine Harrison

Bestseller on Amazon

#50 in Education & Reference> **Study & Teaching**
#76 in Education & Reference > **Instruction**

WHAT OTHERS ARE SAYING...

Educational theories are always changing but end up sounding similar to those they aim to replace. This book is different, opening up exciting new vistas that show how learning is a fundamentally semiotic (sign-governed) process. It does not simply rename traditional psychological and educational concepts with the terminology of semiotics, rather, it penetrates the essence of the human brain through the template of semiotic theory in order to expose those processes within it that are relevant to how we all learn. The implications are enormous. This is a brilliant book and should be read not only by semioticians and educators, but also by anyone who wants to understand how we learn above and beyond the instinctual biological system with which we are endowed.

—*Marcel Danesi, Professor of Linguistic Anthropology, University of Toronto, author of "Encyclopedic Dictionary of Semiotics, Media, and Communications"*

What does semiotics, often seen as a recondite and abstract theorization of how symbols function, have to say to educators trying to do the difficult job of supporting student learning? Francois Tochon offers us a sampling of practical teaching and research tools based in semiotic principles that help move education away from fixed methods, best practices, and rigid content standards toward understanding learning as coming at meaning sideways and creatively, always re-defining, re-imagining, and improvising for our own purposes here and now. Educators and education researchers sorely need to learn this lesson.

—*Jay Lemke, Department of Communication, University of California–San Diego; author of "Talking Science: Language, Learning," and "Values and Textual Politics: Discourse and Social Dynamics"*

Learning is meaning-making, in all levels of life. Educational semiotics studies the deep mechanisms of semiosis in learning and teaching processes in humans. Tochon does this in practice.

—Kalevi Kull, Professor of Semiotics, University of Tartu, coauthor of "Towards a Semiotic Biology: Life is the Action of Signs"

Educational Semiotics is a highly original work of scholarship. In four ingeniously designed studies, Francois Tochon demonstrates how semiotic analysis can be used to deconstruct the professional learning experiences of preservice teachers. These studies offer startling insights into the creative application of semiotic methods, the understanding of long standing issues in teacher education, and the nature of learning in situated contexts. Thus, this book is helpful to semioticians, teacher educators, and all those interested in how professionals learn through experience. The genius of Tochon's work is his skillful application of semiotic methods to frame and probe the depths of well-known problems in teacher education, such as how teachers learn through practice. The implications of his work are profound and their potential for further investigation is enormous. In essence, Tochon is pointing the way to a new field of endeavor that he has termed Educational Semiotics.

—John Henning, former President of Semiotics in Education at the American Educational Research Association, Ohio University, author of "Using Action Research to Improve Instruction"

Semiotic inquiry is an ever-evolving construction and work such as Tochon's raises contemporary questions about the search for meaning and the processes through which we make meaning. His work demonstrates that meaning classifications are not products of a static system, but rather dynamic events which reshape their organizing as a continuous process of meaning creation. The four studies in this book are rich, flexible, and reflect critical knowledge transformation. In addition to illustrating new ways to approach semiotic research, Tochon's innovative reasoning insists that we reorganize our intuitive assumptions and reanalyze our insights with regards to our semiotic understandings about learning and teaching.

—Elvira Katić, Executive Director of the Semiotic Society of America, Associate Professor of Education, Ramapo College of New Jersey, author of "Technology and the Inner Eye"

Contents

Foreword by Gary Shank	9
Preamble	11
Introduction. The Role of Semiotics in Education Inquiry	13
Signs Shape our Belief Systems	14
Research as Transformation	15
Rich, Flexible, non-Essentializing Inquiry	17
Synthesizing Binaries	19
Categories as Temporary Attempts	20
Semiotic Mapping as Ontological Design	21
Peirce's Analytical Framework	23
Organization of the Book	24
Study 1. Semiotic Mapping as Source of Knowledge Transformation for Student Teachers	29
Methodology	31
Harun, Student Teacher 1	34
Esra, Student Teacher 2	38
Discussion	46
Study 2. Psychosemiotic Analysis of Reflective Conflict in a Video Study Group	49
Psychosemiotics of Social Interactions and Development	50
Methodology	53
Case Analysis	55
Reflective Equilibrium: A Discussion	61
Study 3. Semiotic Grammar of Educational Portfolios: Student Teachers' Struggles in Researching Best Practice	63
Electronic Portfolios and Quality Teaching	64

Methodology	66
Case Analysis: Computer Enabled Assessment	70
Discussion	74
Conclusion	79
Study 4. When Authentic Experiences are Framed into Instructional Genres	**83**
The Theoretical Issues	87
From subject-matter knowledge to actualization	89
Methodology	98
Authentic experiences in language learning	100
Beyond disciplinary genres: When learning is othernessing	106
In Summary	109
Conclusion. The Benefits of Semiotic Mapping	**113**
Glossary	**117**
References	**123**
Deep Education Press: Scientific Board Members	134
Author's Biosketch	136
Correspondence	137

Also by François Victor Tochon

Tropics of Teaching: Productivity, Warfare, and Priesthood. Toronto, ON: University of Toronto Press

Help Them Learn a Language Deeply! The Deep Approach to World Languages and Cultures. Blue Mounds, WI: Deep Education Press.

Tochon, F. V., & Busciglio D. F. *Eds.* (2017). *Deep Education Across the Disciplines and Beyond: A 21st Century Breakthrough.* Blue Mounds, WI: Deep Education Press.

Nowadays the importance of education has emerged hand in hand with the complexity of the means of communication, the evolution of the labor market, and the impacts of information technology on consumerism; yet there is an overall lack of understanding about the goal of contemporary education. Professor Tochon's book offers us a thorough semiotic inquiry of this matter, deeply investigating how knowledge transfer is possible only through the generation of meaning. *Educational Semiotics* goes beyond the conventional reflections on the optimization of learning, demonstrating the power and capacity of applied semiotics to reveal the deep transformative nature of education. Education itself is the most intensive process of semiosis.

—**Kristian Bankov, Professor of Semiotics, New Bulgarian University, Sofia**

Foreword

Gary Shank
Duquesne University

In this monograph on Educational Semiotics, Francois Tochon (along with a number of research colleagues) has produced a work that is truly groundbreaking on a number of fronts. First of all, in his concise but brilliant introductory comments, Tochon clearly debunks the potential notion that semiotics might provide yet another methodological tool in the toolkit of educational researchers. Drawing skillfully on the work of Peirce, Deely, Sebeok, Merrell, and others, Tochon shows us just how fundamentally different semiotic research can be when compared to the modes and techniques that have dominated educational research for many decades. That is, he points out how semiotic methods can provide the capability for both students and researchers to look at this basic and fundamental human process in inescapably transformational ways, by acknowledging and accepting that the path to knowledge is, in his words "through the fixation of belief."

But he does not stop there – instead, in four brilliantly conceived studies, he shows us how semiotic concepts in general, and semiotic mapping in particular, can allow both student teachers and researchers alike insights in these students' development of insights and concepts into the very heart of the teaching and learning process.

By tackling both theoretical and practical research considerations, Tochon has provided the rest of us the beginnings of a blueprint that, if adopted, can push educational research out of (in the words of Deely) its entrenchment in the Age of Ideas into the new and exciting frontiers of the Age of Signs.

10

Preamble

This monograph is a follow-up to the doctoral seminar in Educational Semiotics organized at the University of Wisconsin–Madison in the Fall of 2012. It was published as a reader companion to the 2013 XIXth School of Semiotics held in September in the old beautiful seaside town of Sozopol in Bulgaria; on behalf of the Southeast European Center for Semiotics Studies in the New Bulgarian University of Sofia-Bulgaria, in collaboration with the Departments of New Bulgarian studies, Advertising and Marketing, Applied Linguistics, Cognitive Sciences, Philosophy and Sociology, Visual Arts, Theatre, Drama and Cinema. It became the basis for a Seminar in Educational Semiotics, shared with Gary Shank, at the Semiotic Society of America 2013 Conference.

I am grateful to numerous semioticians who have guided me and become friends during the last thirty years who have all contributed to my current understanding of Educational Semiotics, a field in which a great many avenues need further exploration. It was Marc Eigeldinger, Jean Rychner and Eddy Roulet in Neuchâtel who first introduced me to Ferdinand de Saussure's semiology, Algirdas Greimas's semiotic square, Roland Barthes, and French and American semiotics. I started to read Thomas Sebeok in the seventies, dreaming that maybe one day I could be visiting Indiana-Bloomington. I could not imagine at the time that later in my life I would teach in the U.S. and meet the authors I did appreciate so much. In particular, I remember a critical presentation of the Oracle of Delphi at Purdue by Tom Sebeok, Marcel Danesi's appearances at the American Educational Research Association (AERA) while we were coediting the International Journal of Applied Semiotics (IJAS), or when he visited our home in Madison and started accompanying my wife

Isabelle on the piano playing the air of Brindisi in the Traviata. I also remember the discussion of Peter McLaren on the semioticized Self and its social transformation when he had just arrived at UCLA; Linda Rogers' life stories; Ricki Goldman's video constellations at UBC; and Nancy Stockall's, John Henning's, Marcy Driscoll and John Rausch's help while I was in charge of the Special Interest Group of Semiotics in Education at AERA. I am also very grateful to Linda Babler at Atwood Publishing for her practical contribution to applied semiotics and her help in publishing IJAS. For all these years, I had the pleasure of hearing Deborah Smith-Shank on visual culture, gender and semiotic pedagogy; Liora Bresler on the taste of music; Michael Silverstein on the wine-talk registers; and Stanton Wortham on the Shakespearean play in the classroom.

My field of application is related to world languages and cultures. I always felt second language acquisition to be a quite narrow field of study. When one works in applied semiotics, applied linguistics seems to relate to language without the soul. Semantics lacks an interpretant. This is why I was most pleased to see Richard Young consulting colleagues in Madison on his 2010 keynote lecture of the American Association for Applied Linguistics (AAAL): he demonstrated the need to integrate semiotics in the vision.

The last but not the least—I am most grateful to the preservice teachers who participated in the three first studies. Study 1 was supported by a grant from Tübitak—the National Science and Technology Council of Turkey—and from the Spencer Foundation. Elif Kir, research assistant, helped with some aspects of data collection and transcription. Thanks go to Münire Erden for her support all along the implementation of the portfolio project in Turkey. For the third study, my warmest thanks go to Steve Head, UW director of Educational Portfolios and Career Services (EPCS) for his e-portfolio support along the last five years. Finally, I am indebted to the Social Sciences and Humanities Research Council of Canada, which funded Study 4.

Introduction

The Role of Semiotics in Education Inquiry

François Victor Tochon

Educational Semiotics is intended for researchers, university faculty, teacher educators, and graduate students in education, and more broadly for anyone interested in how knowledge is broadened using semiotic inquiry for a deeper understanding of educational processes.

Educational semiotics is applied semiotics with a purpose[1]. Semiotics is useful to Education in two respects: it first can be crucial for a better grasp and exploration of education practices, which may lead to better, deeper and more meaningful practices; second it can inform deeper ways of researching education as a field for which signs and sign processes are needed.

Readers who need an introduction to semiotics might want to read John Deely's (1990) *Basic of Semiotics*, Daniel Chandler (2007) *Semiotics: The basics*, Paul Cobley's (2009) *Routledge Companion to Semiotics*, or consult Marcel Danesi's (2000) *Encyclopedic Dictionary of Semiotics, Media, and Communications*. Students often appreciate as well the clear and well-contextualized explanations of Floyd Merrell (2000) in *Change through signs of body, mind, and language,* and Danesis'

---

[1] Part of this introduction was published in Tochon (2009a) in the *International Applied Semiotics Journal* with the title: Semiotic Inquiry or the Advent of Deep Methodologies.

(1999) wit in *Of Cigarettes, High Heels, and Other Interesting Things*, a reminder of George Lakoff's (1987) *Women, Fire, and Dangerous Things*.

Signs Shape our Belief Systems

Semiotics is the study of semiosis[2] or sign action; it can describe any process that includes the production of meaning, whether linguistic or not. Thus semiosis defines the process of making meaning as mediated by signs and the interpretation of those signs. Curricula constitute applied semiotics for the purpose of Education; their enactments lead to educational semiosis. Significantly, teachers' awareness of semiosis generates *metasemiosis* (Urban, 2006), as their engagement in such deep reflection stimulates conceptual reframing, which can be qualified itself as a trans-semiotic process. Metasemiosis was explored by John Deely, Susan Petrilli and Augusto Ponzio (1998), Thomas Sebeok (2001), and scholars who referred to the human as a 'metasemiotic animal', able to generate meaning-making on meaning-making. From intuiting to perceiving to wording, stages of clarification operate what Charles S. Peirce (1877a) has deciphered and theorized as being inherent to the process of belief confirmation that characterizes scientific inquiry. In a similar manner, intuiting, perceiving and wording curriculum interpretations involves a subtle belief formation that the studies in this book aim to explore through mapping curriculum processes in learning, teaching, and teacher education.

Peirce defined science as the process of fixing beliefs. Belief systems are the substrates of meanings sedimented by habits that crystallized into knowledge. In a similar way, curriculum inquiry is led by genuine doubt on the ground of belief cultures. The inquiry process gives opportunities for deeper interaction with a variety of possible meanings, and it furthers the development of understanding. Peirce proposed four ways of fixing beliefs: tenacity, authority, a priori, and experiment (1877b).

---

[2] See Glossary proposed at the end of the book.

Experimentation was his preferred way to provide negotiation, cooperation, and openness to alternatives. Peirce's work thus helps provide a framework to understand teacher beliefs and more generally education. Experimentations provide teachers ways to investigate and alter their beliefs. Genuine revision of prior judgments is a constant process and requires a new vision of Education and assessment.

Research as Transformation

Within the perspective of semiotic inquiry (Shank, 1995), Education researchers won't partition sign meanings but conceive of the sign's interactional nature within a fluid, social and cultural flow of integrated meaning-making processes. Research can be extended to what I name trans-semiosis in practice, that is a transformational understanding of one's own semiosis (Tochon & Okten, 2010). Semiotics plays a deciphering and hermeneutic role in highlighting the organizing of and contradictions in discourse and any form of communication, and may offer methodologies that respond to the challenges met by current educational research. In his 'Theory of Signs'—which is a presentation of Peirce's mature theory of semiosis—Short (2007) reiterates that sign processing (semiosis) is infinite and happens whereby something comes to signify something else to somebody or any system that can be informed by a sign.

Research methods have much to learn from semiotics (Shank, 1995). I have been teaching research methods courses for the last 18 years and have become acutely aware that sound research is much more than respecting a method. I obviously need to teach graduate students to be in the academic survival mode-that is, respecting genres and methodological canons. However I feel that one of the current duties of experienced researchers is to break the genres and open the field of educational research to broader semiotics.

Along this line of thought, the third Handbook of Qualitative Research (Denzin & Lincoln, 2005) was a breakthrough. It rejected "the falsity of a supposed research-activism dualism with *research* seen as dispassionate, informed and rational, and with *activism* seen as passionate, intuitive, and weakly theorized" (p.569 italics mine). Indeed sustaining the myth of the researcher detached from social practices is risky. The exploration of social praxis and its environment from a methodological perspective may obscure the conceptual motives that underlie the choice of methods. For instance, contemplate the clash in perspective between conversation analysis (CA)—a research method with no apparent epistemological claim—and critical discourse analysis (CDA), which manifests critical epistemologies with no apparent methodological claim. This is but a reminder of the debate between Feyerabend (1975), Lakatos & Musgrave (1980) on methods as a possible barrier to scientific discovery.

Postmodern Lather (2008) reemphasized this aspect. Depending upon the epistemological and ontological choices, the description of method clashes with the conceptual framework, as a betrayal of the original intent. Teaching research through methods is a structuralist approach, with its inevitable reductionisms and a-contextual features. This aspect appears quite important for a better recognition of applied semiotics in Education. Sebeok and later Danesi (2006) suggested that a system view could reconcile the Saussurians and the Peirceans with a shared modeling. Applied Semiotics certainly involves an understanding of complex system dynamics (Larsen-Freeman, 2012).

In any case, another revolution is starting with the understandings that semiotic brings to educational inquiry. I can only allude here to the seminal work of Deely (2007 and 2009) questioning objectivity from both a premodern and postmodern perspective, as subjective perception is inevitably enmeshed in objective experience. This is but a clear indication that semiotics has a message other than modern science and has the potential to subsume its binaries. We are shifting to a new period of human thought, which will legitimate new forms of inquiry. With the understanding that any knowledge implies a fixation of beliefs, the search for meaning is extended to all processes through which humankind evolves toward a better understanding of its humanity. Social inquiry acquires new depth in this complex endeavor that conjugates subtle categories of signs through post-Cartesian reasoning modes. Gary Shank is one of the heirs of Charles S. Peirce. In his forthcoming book *The Semiotic Inquirer in the Age of Signs*, he uncovers stratifications of meaning that have not been explored so far even in the most subtle qualitative studies.

There is a dilemma for journal editors who receive original, creative or critical works that cannot be easily included within the mainstream tone, genre and structures that are common in their volumes. They send such papers to reviewers like hot potatoes, with not much hope that they might fit in their normative constraints. In academic publishing, form has become more importance than meaning and depth. Often space makes it impossible for a researcher to describe why he or she cannot get along with a particular obedience and why often methods impose a formalism that prevents the expression of genius or, more casually said, why sometimes 'methods stink'. For example, methods may be one way to conform to a knowledge industry that is highly normative, prevents epistemological innovation and maintains the status quo. The semiotic reader knows about the debate around Peirce's article on "The fixation of belief". Along this line of thought, Habermas (1995) suggested that facts are social norms, as they have a shared interpretive dimension. Inquiry is most often circumscribed into research gates. Moreover the claim for research neutrality serves an ideological function that justifies the interests and status of the wealthy and the dominant.

Rich, Flexible, non-Essentializing Inquiry

Feedback is always interesting inasmuch as it reveals a lot about yourself and so much about your reviewers. It has been common practice in the semiotics field to accommodate authors in the blossoming of their thought and the idea of rejecting the proposal of an academically qualified researcher is excruciating and always difficult to bear. Semiotic criteria tend to keep a non-essentializing character. In this realm, there is still much to investigate, question, and discover. First we need a better definition of semiotic inquiry. The search for meaning does not only elicit the cultural role of education but also transforms its process (Shank, 1995): the researcher's skepticism helps her discover potential truths "through successive stages of dissatisfaction", which actually entails an endless postponement of the fixation of belief (Short, 2007, p.331).

The aim of semiotic inquiry evolves. It involves a variety of approaches that confer richness and flexibility in the signifying stages of perception, feeling and reasoning. The discovery process creates new languages and changes existing languages in a transformative semiosis (Bopry, 2002). The evolving viewpoint becomes integrative, as it resolves the reasoning binaries of the modern split.

Semiotic inquiry integrates the revision of its aims, whatever the aims of inquiry. The sense of possible truth gradually develops, from authority towards a sense of what naturally coheres that leads, eventually, to what experience compels us to believe. This last view only establishes a certain sense of truth, independent yet fluid and dynamic rather than fixed and naturalized. There is a human tendency to settle on established convictions: human meanings match perceptual patterns of perception. The sphere of meaning-making poses boundary conditions that define semiotic niches within meaning environment systems (or *Umwelten*, reviewed by Agamben, 2004). Semiotics provides a dynamic point of view rather than a simple method of fixing beliefs (W3: 248). It creates its methodological antidote as it deconstructs its own semiotic process.

In this demonstration lies another paradox. Since semiotic discussion is wide-ranging and so heterogeneous—with such fluidity in the discovery of anything deemed to be potentially permanent—it can't possess basic concepts (or a common dictionary), opines Simpkins (2001). Despite a number of consensual semiotic constructs such as semiosis, denotation, firstness, context, signified, interpretant, shared among semioticians, the nature of the field would require—Simpkins claims—that no basic construct be posited as the ultimate semiotic truth and relevance principle. Nonetheless, as in the fluidization or 'anti-fixation of belief', conceptual tools don't hinder the semiotician from re-conceptualizing their situated, local dynamics. The life sphere is permeated by semiosis and meaning, and the understanding of its holographic nature fixes syllogism and its paradox.

Synthesizing Binaries

While Simpkins (2001) suggested that semiotics needs to be disentangled from structuralism and its essentializing or naturalizing of constructs, I would posit that structural analysis is but one interpretive and insufficient dimension that always needs to be complemented with the description of how the componential items that are being deciphered are recomposed, reshaped and challenged within the semiotic dynamics of social and possibly cross-cultural semiosis. Semioticians need to resolve the challenging contrast between the semiotic, structural attempt, and the post-semiotic, critical dynamics. Both coexist as one, as the yin and the yang of situated meaning making. These two views are paradigmatically opposed- however, they could be reconciled if one considered them as two faces of any attempt at deciphering reality: the static description of the ontological structure that relies upon molar, symbolic units is being moderated through the antagonistic description of their dynamics (or epistemic processes) in local semiotic encounters, which are paradoxically both unique and plural. As well the local dynamics can encompass the social factor and make semiosis a social enterprise. Meaning is embedded in a diversity of systems of reason in constant exchange. Constance is in change. Interchange semiosis redirects semiotics towards considering the dynamics of local exchanges among different meaning systems. It entails that we can extend the perspective and consider local cultures, including those of which existence is denied, and re-conceptualize discourse decoding from the viewpoint of its coherence vis-à-vis ethical goals that would give discourse and action their real meaning in the long run.

Semiosis or the sign meaning-making process is clearly described by Charles Sanders Peirce to be the fluid and moving interplay of signifiers, signified and interpretants whose iterative roles may be exchanged (Merrell, 2000; Bains, 2006). In biosemiotics for instance, Hoffmeyer (2008) suggests that autopoiesis and self-reference, code binarity, the use of receptors, and endosemiosis are inherent properties of living systems. Positing such basic concepts or lexicon, which contrasts with Simkins's (2001) position, does not entail that the components that induce semiosis are context-independent. The ontological dilemma for semiotic theory is the limitation of the symbolic model if sign units are considered independent from their context. Most processes in nature, from the cell to the ecosystem, that can be conceptualized as sign-processes are context-dependent. Life-processes are part of semiotic dynamics. The sign-aspects of the processes of life define specific, local semiospheres, beams of situated meaning in pragmatic worlds of communication.

Categories as Temporary Attempts

Semioticians need to create a more complete account and fuller picture of the sign dynamics that include humane practice and the chaotic, interpersonal nature of meaning construction and exchange for education purposes. Using atomic physics as an analogy, we can conceive of signs as either corpuscles of meaning or pragmatic waves depending on the focus. Taxonomized categories provide one dimension of semiotic theorizing only and infinite semiosis prevails.

Instead of viewing categories of meaning as produced by a static system, we should conceive of how events dialogically reshape their organizing into a dynamic and continuous process of meaning creation. Thus, "ultimately the *events* are what the term *language* labels" (Stewart, 1995, p.112 italics mine). In Steward's post-semiotic theory—which adopts some Wittgensteinian stands—language is constitutive. This understanding places humans in face of their responsibilities. Indeed if human semiosis constructs and develops the educational world, then this precise understanding demands that we connect discourse and action proactively to their ethical and ontological consequences (Kristeva, 1991), shifting the semiotic endeavor toward a *felt* endeavor with a slow-motion analysis of the grounds for educational discourse and action. Critiquing Education discourse and action leads to a broader understanding of how human situations acquire meaning vis-à-vis larger, ethical goals relating to Deep Education principles.

Such endeavor would always be tentative and in process. It would go along with a conception of educational semiotics that does not propose structurally-fixed and fundamental constituents of meaning as they are always dialogically re-constructed and are limited to be partial representations of possible world views. Critical semiotics challenges its own interpretations, applying principles such as Kristeva's (1991): the reading of signs must be complemented by a skeptical awareness of the slipperiness of meaning uses. Accessing the semiotic dimensions—which are conveyed by the enunciation style of utterances, the situational events and pragmatic struggles and their context—kindles social critique. "According to Kristeva, what society systematically represses provides clues to what is oppressive about society and how society needs to be changed. Thus, she discerns a vital ethical potential in the semiotic" (Stanford Encyclopedia of Philosophy, 2004).

> . . . we have no knowledge a priori of how to inquire -- there can never be a time when we will know, for sure, that we are proceeding in the right way or even that there is a right way to proceed. We can only go by the evidence we have so far acquired, in faith that there is an impersonal truth, that is, a final opinion toward which an ideal inquiry would tend. The evidence that supports that faith is extensive and compelling and yet conceivably erroneous. It is shot through with

uncertainty, unanswered questions, unresolved problems, and vague formulations. (Short, 2007, p.347)

Personal truths are perfectible and can evolve toward becoming dialogical and inter-subjective. Such stabilization of evidential faith eventually and inevitably fossilizes and requires further semiosis.

Semiotic Mapping as Ontological Design

Conceptual mapping requires a support for communication, such as an economic organigram, planning rubric, literary genealogy, geographic representation, anthropological card, systems representation, linguistic tree, semantic structure, cognitive frame, mental model, sociological tree of knowledge. Such visual maps constitute ontologies or conceptual systems that model 'what is'. When designing such models of reality, then, students are involved in an epistemic process, a way of conceptualizing disciplinary priorities. Therefore conceptual maps are sometimes named epistemic maps. Several excellent and thorough reviews have been published on concept mapping (Brown, 2002; Daley et al., 1999; Danesi, 2002; Gómez et al., 2000; Goodyear et al., 2005; Novak & Cañas, 2008; Tochon, 1990).

Peirce had been alerted early about the merits of diagrammatic mapping as a way to support and enhance logical reasoning and represent the Mind (CP 4.582). His 'existential graphs', published in 1906 (CP 4.618) had been invented in 1897, as he mentioned, and probably even earlier. Peirce created rules for reasoning with diagrams as a means of helping experiment with thought and investigate the logical relationships between concepts. Peirce tried to improve his system of concept mapping for more than 20 years and was not really satisfied with his logical, 'gamma graphs' at the end of his life. Nonetheless he considered that 'all necessary reasoning is diagrammatic' (Draft C, 90-102) that is, any conceptualizing is a mapping process. His purpose was 'to illustrate the general course of thought: (...) a system of diagrammatization by means of which any course of thought can be represented with exactitude' (CP 4.530). Each 'phemic sheet' would represent a universe of discourse as 'icons of intelligible relations' (CP 4.531). Øhrstrom (1997) indicates that diagrammatical reasoning is semiotically very powerful, yet as any representation it can't be perfect or complete: it provides a viewpoint. Practical reasoning might not follow the rules of mathematical logic or might embody another mathematical field (Menand, 1997): the logic of 'moving pictures of thought' (CP 4.8).

Since Peirce proposed his existential graphs, much work has been done to develop logical maps that provide precise representations of ways of reasoning and fields of knowledge. Student teachers' revisiting of their own concept maps makes them aware of differences between their concepts. Such structures make students ascertain what they know about their educational experience. The learner's structure of understanding becomes precise and clear, which indicates their role in the essentializing, naturalizing process of school meanings. The study of how curriculum knowledge is transformed into something that can be handled in practice provides interesting indications on the interpretation of school notions and genres presented and processes described by the students (Tochon, 2000b). Such maps can be used to observe the initial stages of a learner's knowledge as well as monitor conceptual changes. Curriculum mapping can be a method that makes students acquire 'a habit of changing habits' (Kankkunen, 2004, p.1). It allows both student teachers and teachers to evaluate their conceptual development and belief system.

To sum up, concept mapping research can be extended to subtle processes which imply a transformational understanding of one's own semiosis. Semiotic curriculum inquiry thus defined can be integrated into teacher education to stimulate the ability of student teachers to reflect on their curriculum knowledge and the meaning making process more broadly. The next section digs into this analytical framework further.

Peirce's Analytical Framework

For Peirce (1931-1958), logic has to be interpreted in its contextual dynamics; the context of an utterance conditions its interpretation. Any interpretable movement, or any thought is a sign (Chandler, 2003). Meanings are constructed to form realities, culture, and communication. Peirce's model of signs depicts the agency components of meaning constructions in the reciprocal movement of signs, objects and interpretants. The sign mediates between the object and its interpretant. The interpretant is the interpretive outcome of the sign which indicates that different signs may reference different aspects of an object, leading to different outcomes or effects. As deduction and induction are not capable of generating new knowledge, a third inferential process creates hypotheses and instructional guesses: abductive reasoning moves from the interpretive result to the rule to the case (Bopry, 2002).

As we move from abduction (or intuition) to deduction through a phase of induction, we progress from the simple reconciliation of meaning toward the prescribed process of selecting the necessary truth (Shank, 1995). The Peircean model characterizes the semiotic process on the basis of three movements of meaning making: firstness, secondness and thirdness. Firstness (or idea-representamen) is associated with qualities that have an iconic relationship with their objects (a photograph, portrait, map, etc.). Secondness (or brute actuality-object) comes in the recognition of 'the other'. It is the recognition that there is self and not self, and comes into play in the separation of field and ground, given that the nature of secondness is opposition. Firstness involves abduction – which is the spontaneous and direct emergence of meaning – and deals with the person's qualitative ideas and beliefs. Secondness involves induction through verbal and non-verbal signs that the person already experienced consciously. Thirdness associates firstness and secondness through reasoning and making connections, and it is deductive. Thirdness (or a sign's soul-interpretant) refers to the use of symbols. A symbol is a form of thirdness (such as waving hands, traffic lights, etc.). The symbol mediates between an object and the interpretant through law or reason. Semiosis is thus part of the perceptual process, response to the environment dynamics (or *Umwelt* – Deely, 1994).

Organizing perceptions are the ground of learning experience and, in turn, education organizes perceptions. According to Cunningham, human semiosis and education are but one and the same thing. 'If by semiosis we mean the lifelong building of structures of experience, then education is precisely that field which attempts to understand, nurture and make people more reflective about this process' (Cunningham, 1987, p.207). Thus educational perception is formed through semiosis. The process of conceptualizing the curriculum is inferential. The results of this process contribute to the perception of knowledge. In Cunningham's (2002) view, reflexivity is the awareness of semiosis.

Organization of the Book

What do language classroom performances communicate? Like the circus semiotics that Bouissac analyzed in 2011, they attest to professional skills and clever staging. All four studies presented in this book relate to technology applications used by students and student teachers. Katic (2008) showed that deciphering the conceptions of technology held by preservice teachers is one way to help student teachers and their educators construct transformative learning encounters where understandings can be constructively scaffolded or staged into clever and relevant pedagogical choices.

This monograph is a modest opening to the broad field of educational semiotics. It gathers the excerpts of four studies that illustrate why semiotics brings crucial understanding of educational processes. In the four studies presented here, we use three ways of mapping educational understandings: the first study shows how to use a Peircean analysis in part due to his work with existential diagrams, making his theories a natural match for concept maps; the second and third studies use Greimas's actantial mapping as way of deciphering the story grammar of student teacher experiences; and the fourth study uses a Saussurian diagram and a heuristic schema to highlight the differences between (*diachronic*) instructional planning and its (*synchronic*) actualizing. One after the other we reinvest these concepts into theorizing the curriculum semiotic process. Curriculum mapping can stimulate semiotic inquiry and student teachers' transformation of knowledge.

Concept mapping has often been interpreted within a classical cognitive framework, a framework that fixes semantic meanings instead of situating the pragmatics of the interpretive flow that characterizes learning trans-semiosis like we did here. The *first study* of the book focuses on the way student teachers try to grasp curriculum organizing through semiotic diagrams or concept maps. When a student teacher maps her sense of the annual curriculum, she has to organize her intuitive assumptions about what is hierarchically important and visualize it. In a similar way, the reader of a curriculum map must let hypotheses and assumptions emerge from the visuals. Then, through induction the construction of assumptions takes place (Kankkunnen, 2004). Thereafter, through deduction the meanings of such assumptions are interpreted and knowledge is dynamically designed.

The *second study* proposes a psychosemiotic view of reflective conflict in video study groups organized in preservice education. The video study group provides a flexible coming together of student teachers involved in semiotic inquiry on their own actions and professional contexts, with the goal of professional development. The psychosemiotic framework is employed to analyze the degrees to which resulting reflective conflicts lead to adopting life-long professional developmental actions in affordance with students' learning.

The *third study* examines the semiotic grammar of educational portfolios to see how student teachers make sense of the integration of new technologies in their teaching. Indeed for preservice teachers attempting to utilize technology in classroom settings, developing this environmental responsiveness is an area of struggle. Palacio-Cayetano, Schmier, Dexter, and Stevens (2002) found that preservice teachers lag behind experienced in-service teachers in conceptualizing how technology must be adapted to—rather than be imposed upon—a classroom context. Student teachers prefer teacher-centered uses of technology (Wang, 2002). Meskill, Mossop, DiAngelo & Pasquale (2002) further note the difficulty preservice teachers using technology have in focusing on student learning, adapting activities when technical difficulties arise, and in organizing student-centered, process-oriented learning. On a related note, similar integrative dissonance is also evident as preservice teachers develop their portfolios (Breault, 2004). They risk becoming glossy showcases while substance and reflection should be the focus.

The goal of the *fourth study* is to show how experience transcends subject-matter planning, and the paradoxical nature of planning for authentic experiences. Subject matters are semiotically defined here as instructional genres. They are integrated into a new framework for semiotic research into curriculum and instruction under the banner of European didactics (explained hereafter) as a prototype discipline. The data that serve as the basis for what the study demonstrates relate to oral communication in elementary-level learning groups (groups of 9-year-olds). An analytic model is presented which indicates the reciprocal influence of the premises for action and situated links in learning.

The studies presented in this monograph are contributions to a better understanding of teacher learning through the in-depth analysis of student teachers' educational narratives—at the time of organizing their curriculum, during classroom interactions, and in video study groups while they are reflecting on their practice—and to the integration of videos and electronic portfolios for awareness raising and the analysis of teacher experiential narratives. Educational semiotics in each case contributed to a deeper account of educational processes.

To sum up, this monograph explores the semiotic basis for specific forms of educational inquiry that can stimulate *metasemiosis*, generating meaning-making on meaning-making. As a semiotic tool, curriculum concept mapping can initiate a transformative semiosis of semiosis, a process we name trans-semiosis. *Trans-semiosis* is the transformation of knowledge that results from the reframing process of metasemiosis, and make the process transformative. Since trans-semiosis is so closely related to the dialogical understanding of self and the other – and knowledge is not distinct from the semiosis process – it results that trans-semiosis is an identity process.

STUDY 1

Semiotic Mapping as a Source of Knowledge Transformation for ELT[1] Student Teachers

François Victor Tochon and Celile Eren Ökten

EXCERPTS FROM

Tochon, François Victor and Ökten, Celile E., (2010). Curriculum mapping and instructional affordances: Sources of transformation for student teachers. *Transnational Curriculum Inquiry,* 7 (1). Retrieved from:
http://nitinat.library.ubc.ca/ojs/index.php/tci

In this Study, we discuss semiosis, metasemiosis, knowledge emergence and generation processes through three types of reasoning: abduction, induction, and deduction. Education can be viewed as a semiotic process of deciphering that co-constructs meaningful relations between one learner or a group of learners, the curriculum and the teacher. This understanding brings a humane dimension to the education process. We will see how reasoning provides meaning to signs, allowing for interpretations and inferences. The last step, based on the production of meaning, is to explore how perception is structured by education on the basis of experience. For that purpose, we present a taxonomy that will help us analyze student teachers' perceptions related to curriculum mapping.

Semiotic theory offers a broad framework to understand

---

[1] ELT: English Language Teaching (as a Foreign Language)

curriculum meaning making processes and to highlight the subtle progressions between implicit stages and more explicit stages of understanding within perception itself. Peirce devised ten classes of signs as part of his theory. In the terminology proposed by Merrell (2000), this taxonomy includes: a) Feeling (Peirce's *qualisign*); b) Imaging (*iconic sinsign*); c) Sensing (*rhematic indexical sinsign*); d) Awaring (*dicent sinsign*); e) Scheming (*iconic legisign*); f) Impressing-saying (*rhematic indexical legisign*); g) Looking (Acknowledging)-Saying (*dicent indexical legisign*); h) Seing (Identifying)-Saying (*rhematic symbol*); i) Perceiving-Saying (*dicent symbol or proposition*); and j) Realizing (*argument*) (MS 540, CP 2.233-72). Shank & Cunningham (1996) derived from Peirce's taxonomy six distinct modes for abduction, complemented by three inductive modes and one mode for deduction (Cunningham, 1998; Cunningham, Arici, Schreiber & Lee, 2002), sketched out as follows:

1. The **Hunch** type of inference opens awareness to the virtual possibility of a possible resemblance: initial observations might serve as intuitive suggestions for possible evidence.

2. **Symptoms** would appeal to possible resemblances, comparing properties to be considered, looking for the presence of a more general phenomenon. The detection of a symptom often implies a dependence on prior experience.

3. **Metaphor or Analogy** manipulates resemblance to create new, potential rules and conceptual frames.

4. The **Clue** would lead to the type of inference dealing with possible evidence, a mode of determining whether or not observations are clues of some more general phenomenon. The sign would help detect the circumstances of a past state of affairs. In order to make a judgment, the observer would look for connections.

5. The **Diagnosis or Scenario** forms a possible rule on the basis of available evidence, in order to discover diagnostic judgments amidst observations. Such diagnoses create

plausible scenarios from the cluster of clues. The patterns of clues take on a unity of character.

6. **Explanations** concern formal rules to account for puzzling clusters of data and gather scenarios into a coherent explanation that forms the basis for meaningful insight.

7. **Identification**. Inductive inference testing for the actual evidence of a particular thing, examining if an observation is an instance of the phenomenon under investigation. This might be called construct validation.

8. **Prediction**. Induction of a probable rule through actual evidence, testing the veracity of a hypothetical and possibly causal relationship.

9. **Model building**. Models are being built when inductive testing leads to a probable conclusion based upon a set of rules. Rules then form a coherent chain of reasoning from which actual experience can be tested, from which worldviews can emerge.

10. **Formal reasoning**. Reasoning in which a necessary conclusion is reached based upon formal deductive rules.

This model will help us analyze the capacity of student teachers for 'suspension of action and deliberation for critical thinking and conscious awareness' (Petrilli & Ponzio, 2007, p.7).

Methodology

In this first study, we propose to explicate curriculum mapping as the result of affordances that characterize semiotic inquiry in teacher education.

Setting. This study is one aspect of a larger inquiry that bears on the integration of portfolios in the English Language Teaching (ELT) department of a public university in Istanbul, Turkey. We studied what role e-portfolios could play in the enhancement of teacher education. The aim of the teacher education program was to train culturally learned teachers who have a deep knowledge of their discipline and their profession on the basis of exploratory and participatory action research (Kemmis & McTaggart, 2005). Curriculum mapping was integrated in the portfolio with multiple feedback loops and formative evaluations.

Participants. This study involved 23 volunteer student teachers of English Language Teaching (ELT). They were third year students in a 4-year Teacher Education program. Two participants were chosen for the present study (one female and one male). At some points they allude to a third participant, Seval, whose map is not analyzed here.

Data. The study was based on multiple sources: group discussion, peer work, teacher's participatory observations, oral feedback on their curriculum design, research logs, students' comments, written and oral interviews. The student teachers had no idea about concept mapping before starting their portfolio. The oral interviews were transcribed verbatim, and written interviews were used additionally to form an opinion about their curriculum inquiry.

Procedure. Concept mapping was an integral step in portfolio planning. Student teachers had to envision and map what English Language Teaching entailed in terms of curriculum contents. Curriculum maps offered a nice way to scaffold conceptual supports in this project-based learning through the student teachers' collaborations and their growing knowledge community. The participants' instructions were to detail through concept maps what they knew rather than what they did not know. They had a workshop on concept mapping providing examples of design construction, linking and presentation of diagrams, organigrams, flow charts, heuristic schemata and concept maps. It was decided not to constrain concept mapping with too many rules, of which formalism could restrict the creative flow. They met once a week at the computer laboratory and had another weekly meeting in a normal classroom to discuss the process and contents. Student teachers were free to choose their own framework and format when they mapped their curriculum knowledge. After preparing their own concept maps, they compared their work with their peers and became evaluators of each others' curriculum maps.

Data analysis. We utilized Shank & Cunningham's (1996) model of reasoning – derived from Peirce's works – to explain student teachers' mapping process as an initial step in the creation of their portfolio. The questions addressed the following points: perception of curriculum knowledge; possible conceptual conflicts in the process of building curriculum knowledge; questions raised while choosing relevant knowledge; transformations of knowledge stimulated by the mapping process; criteria for curriculum relevance; ways of categorizing what is important for the field of action; ways the curriculum was politicized by the categories chosen; curriculum and identity development; and transformative learning in the mapping process. These had been part of the reflections that were shared among participants.

Semiotic analysis of the curriculum mapping process. We focused on the answers of two student teachers related to their curriculum mapping. The answers were evaluated in terms of meaning construction; of student teachers' reflection on the subject matter; of their way of categorizing the subject matter; and the semiotic processes that supported deep, transformative thinking involving identity reframing.

Semiotic processes that led student teachers to think more deeply. We analyzed the student teachers' curriculum maps as the progressive sedimentation of layers of understanding that stimulated semiotic inquiry to frame a personal view of the curriculum. It urged them to think deeply about their subject-matter knowledge. What student teachers learned about themselves in this process was to give attention to the meaning and usage of the language. They saw – which surprised them very much – that when they wrote a word on the map, they would immediately remember another subject matter relevant to it. They decided to limit the sub-titles because conceptual fields were related to each other in a certain way. They had to order the subject matter and select what they believed would be worth keeping on their map.

The next section analyzes their conversations, and the oral interviews as well as written remarks they made during the process. The curriculum maps are presented in Figures 1 and 2.

Harun, Student Teacher 1

Hunch: Harun had had no prior experience with concept mapping, and had never thought about his own curriculum knowledge; therefore the selection of valid topics was a demanding task. His intuitions were not clear. In his oral interview, Harun complained about limited time he had for designing his curriculum map. He was trying to organize his thoughts which were fuzzy at this stage. His design incorporated both structural and social aspects of the curriculum.

Symptom: Harun searched the internet for possible designs. He drafted possible forms of maps trying to put titles and sub-titles. He felt confined mostly to the structural aspect, but it helped him remember basic curriculum knowledge and teaching techniques within the discipline. When we observed him, Harun was looking at the design on paper. He tried to put everything on one page, perceived as the most compact design. He preferred a hierarchical composition of topics. Because Harun's concept map structure largely followed the visual patterns that were given to him earlier, it was evident that these framed his knowledge of the discipline.

Metaphor: Observations indicated that Harun's designing process involved naming and ordering ideas within a hierarchy. He used the internet as a reference resource for both choosing curriculum concepts and map designs. Harun designed his map according to samples on the internet and by comparing the results with his peers, and paid more attention to design than to consistency between titles and sub-titles.

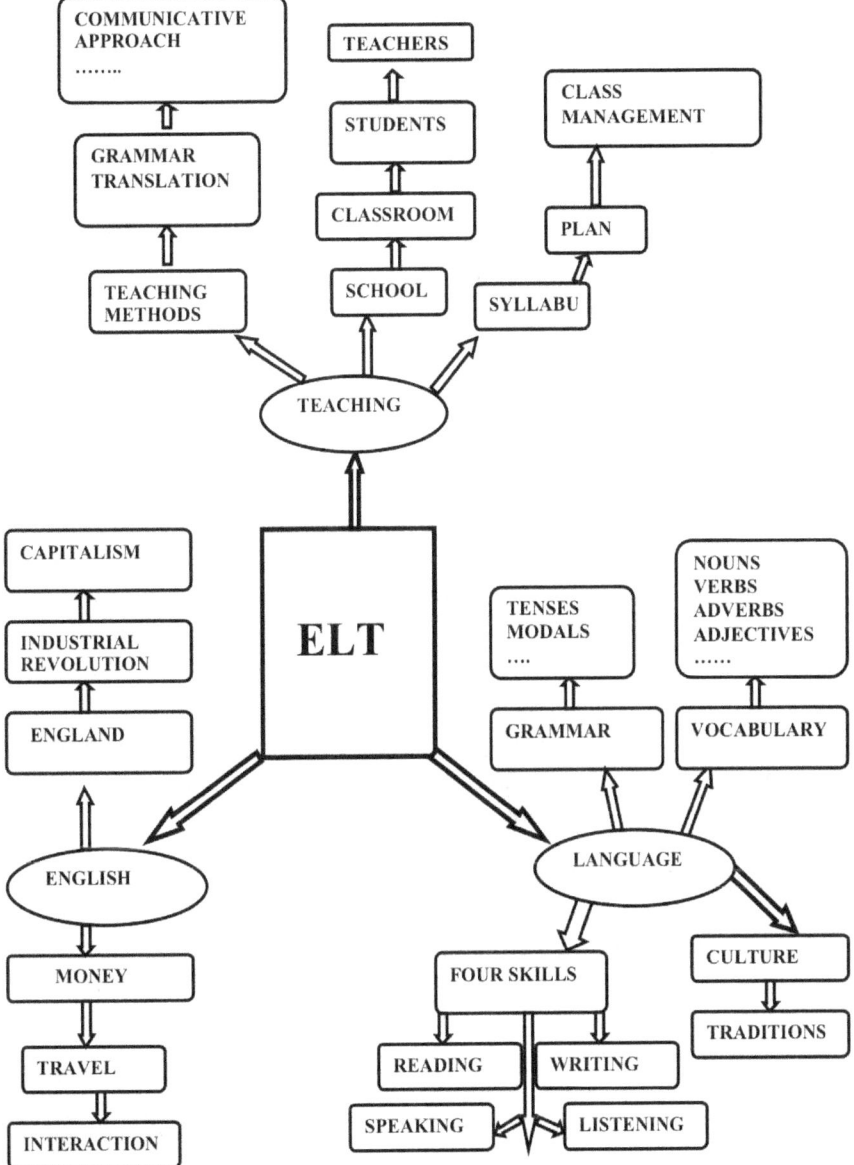

Figure 1. Harun's Curriculum Map

Harun constructed his curriculum knowledge on a structural basis with contents, teaching and learning aspects, and then linked these elements to English- understood as a worldwide language. He also alluded to the historical and economic backgrounds of the discipline. During the interview, Harun did not reflect on the language teaching literature and therefore it did not show up on his concept map, nor did he feel the need to discuss grammar and language skills.

Clue: Harun sees culture as the constructing element of language. He induced how popular English is through its historical importance and current impacts on the economy. He emphasized the social dimension of English as a possible cause for its worldwide popularity. He expressed clearly the connections between teaching and learning.

Diagnosis: Harun states that he used his previous curriculum knowledge in making those connections. Doing his curriculum map was a worthwhile experience. He evaluates concept mapping as a useful method for instruction. For Harun, capitalism and the industrial revolution are primary factors contributing to the popularity of English. To him capitalism is largely the cultural specificity of the Anglo-world: it stimulates its expansion, promotes its hegemony and leads it to control the rest of the world. This diagnostic explains Harun's sub-titles for English language teaching: 'money, travel, and interaction'.

Explanation: Harun clarifies the implications of curriculum mapping: he made a self-assessment of English Language Teaching, and realizes his need to work harder and master the discipline as a whole. The mutual connections between the three different foci of English, Language, and Teaching now become more meaningful to him. Harun could not post more details on his curriculum map because of the size of the paper and, in the electronic format, the size of the webpage. He wanted a hierarchical design that, because of this economy of space, might overlook some topics. The distinctive concepts on his map are 'English', and 'Culture'.

Deductive reasoning: Harun re-read his curriculum map and compared it with his peers, and then made a self-assessment. Knowing English means having advantages in terms of job opportunities. You may earn money more easily, and increase your standard of living. Then you can travel, and interact with other people, and cultures. Thus these dimensions that may motivate learners are key in Harun's curriculum vision. Capitalist power provides currency and characterizes the contributions of English. Harun connects that view with language politics. The power of that currency contributes to shape language policies and education policies around the world. At this point in the creation of the map, Esra intervenes in the conversation and compares her curriculum map with Harun's. She finds his map inadequate, claiming that he needs to write more details about the classroom, language learning, the school environment, and the students. Harun then criticizes himself for not having better exposed issues related to the school, the classroom, and the students, agreeing that such topics should appear more clearly. He also compares his maps with the map of another student teacher Seval. He finds that Seval examines the characteristics of the teacher and learner perspectives in more detail. He especially appreciates her statements about types of learners. Such deductions stimulate his transformative semiosis as he is discovering his own identity traits in the process, which leads him to revise his belief system.

Identification: The next semiosis levels (identification, prediction, and model building) appear clearly in Harun's oral interview. Harun corrects his previous views; he should have written 'Teachers' before the 'Students' title. He had identified these two opposite perspectives coincidentally, but they emphasize different ways of approaching curriculum reality. He responded that he would pay better attention to classroom ecology, and enlarge that topic.

Prediction: The other prospective aspects of what should be learned in English, such as the four skills—grammar, listening, speaking, and writing—are already known and not new topics for

English Language Teaching. Nonetheless Harun still insists on the significance of culture in English learning. The cultural approach should be emphasized and the classroom activities would be better organized along the cultural dimension of the discipline.

Model building: Finally, Harun re-examines ELT through three basic categories: English, Language, and Teaching as expressions of globally constructed curriculum knowledge. This modeling process has been transformative for Harun as he feels a better sense of identification with his curricular stands.

Esra, Student Teacher 2

Hunch: Esra first reflected on her undergraduate program and tried to find examples in her courses at the university. She was wondering what to teach, how to teach, and when to teach. She sailed on sight attempting to figuring out what she knew. She alluded to the contents of courses to which she added her own elements. In the oral interview, Esra remarks that her first concept map was intuitive and disorganized. She wrote down everything coming to her mind; there was no systematic order. Then she started to design another map.

Symptom: Esra drafted her first curriculum map somewhat randomly, and then realized that, after this initial brainstorming, she needed a systematic way of classifying her curriculum knowledge. She built two categories: 'teaching' and 'learning'. She would make a proper selection to match her personal sense of order as necessary along the way. She reflected deeply for a good while, and noticed that certain titles were a good fit as curriculum organizers. One title would remind her of another possible one, and it was an ongoing, creative process. She had to select the most distinctive ones to make English Language Teaching more comprehensible. Indeed ELT related topics such as SLA (second language acquisition), EFL (English as a foreign language), and linguistics were not clear in her mind and would call for more straightfoward theorizing in the discipline. Esra looked for compact curriculum titles that could be flashy in her portfolio and would be noticed immediately. Her primary concerns while designing her concept map were the anticipated result for her e-portfolio. She was heavily geared by her university courses in the choice of contents.

Metaphor: While selecting and writing the sub-titles, Esra pushed herself to limit their number in order to avoid the complexity and messiness of knowledge ramifications. Most of the concepts were related to each other, which allowed her to conclude her selection concisely. 'Language' and 'Teaching' are the main curricular concepts and organizing metaphors. Esra was very interested in language as a science, but paradoxically, she did not really consider linguistics as a relevant category for her map. The categories she chose are important for language learning as an applied field. While she was examining her initial draft, more curriculum categories would come to mind. Then she tried to utilize Bloom's taxonomy in an effort to better organize her map.

Clue: Esra emphasized the present and forthcoming status of English and the importance of the perception that people have of language status, which seemed to explain the role of ELT training in Turkey. If English became less important worldwide, she felt that ELT would be out of the agenda of Turkish education. Esra focused on the language and teaching aspects of ELT. She would not really consider much the topics related to linguistics' and its jargon as, for her, linguistics items were anyway already included in the broader, language category. Esra first considered teaching styles as a category that seemed relevant as a guide for action: in what way would the teacher be a model and, in other words, which characteristics should teachers expose in the classroom? Esra calls the teacher a facilitator, but what does the teacher facilitate in the classroom? She tried to find clues.

Diagnosis: She eventually chose 'linguistics' as well as 'English' as the sub-titles of 'Language' after consulting the maps

ENGLISH LANGUAGE
TEACHING (ELT)
LANGUAGE
Figure 2a
TEACHING
Figure 2b

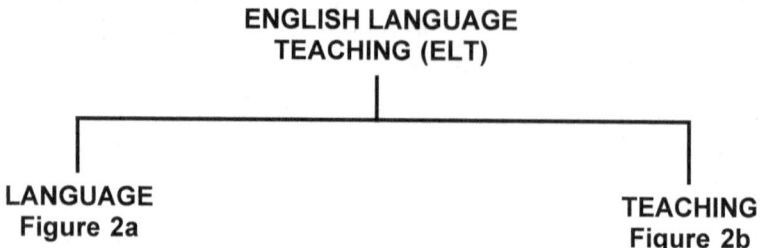

Figure 2. Esra's Curriculum Map

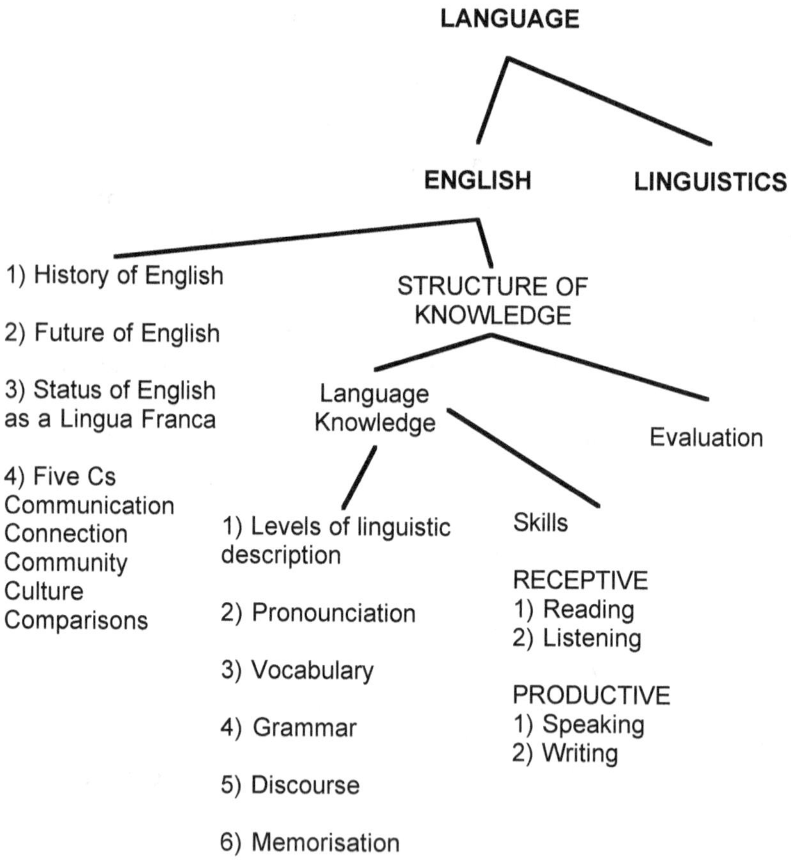

LANGUAGE
ENGLISH
LINGUISTICS
1) History of English
2) Future of English
3) Status of English as a Lingua Franca
4) Five Cs
Communication
Connection
Community
Culture
Comparisons
STRUCTURE OF KNOWLEDGE
Language Knowledge
Evaluation
1) Levels of linguistic description
2) Pronounciation
3) Vocabulary
4) Grammar
5) Discourse
6) Memorisation
Skills
RECEPTIVE
1) Reading
2) Listening
PRODUCTIVE
1) Speaking
2) Writing

Figure 2a. Esra's Curriculum Map

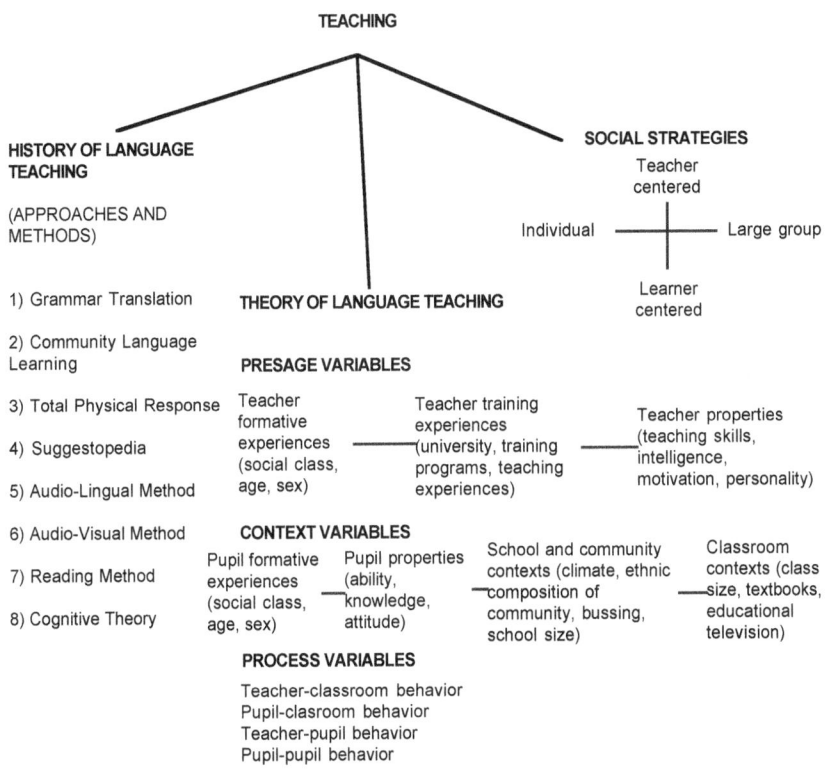

Figure 2b. Esra's Curriculum Map

of her peers. 'History of language teaching', 'theory of language teaching' then became sub-titles of 'teaching'Esra argued that English teaching practices, their historical background, and lingua franca status should be demonstrated during language training, as they were fundamental to the understanding of the discipline. The teacher should orient students towards not only acquiring knowledge, but also interpreting it critically. Besides the general teaching methods such as brainstorming and role-playing, she would distinguish the learner and teacher types separately, and develop the intelligence types as learner characteristics. She thus establishes a diagnostic of useful knowledge.

Explanation: Esra indicated that one might find her curriculum map political, but her attempt was epistemic. For her, teaching the sociocultural aspects was the most crucial in a discipline that otherwise might simply be submitted to hegemonic practices, leading her to question the historical background of English. Today, English seems to be accepted as a lingua franca. Language history would probably help explain to students why they learn English. Esra wants her students to further consider what would happen if they did not learn English, and why English is so popular today rather than other languages? Additionally, Esra examines the status of English, the 5 C's standard approach, instructional materials, social strategies in the classroom, and the language structure in both receptive (interpretive) and productive (presentational) skills). She includes language knowledge and evaluation as crucial elements for teaching English. Esra does not discuss linguistics much because she does not believe it is important for teaching the language. In so doing, her conceptions match communicative theory: she wants to facilitate proficiency, not train grammar specialists.

Deductive reasoning: Having a second look at her map, Esra realized what her real level of English language acquisition was, as well as where she was in terms of her current level of mastery of the theories, classroom applications, and methods. The map helped her reach a level where she could start investigating deductively and systematically into knowledge organizing and proficiency, after the first inductive phases. Curriculum mapping helped Esra remember and reflect deeply on her disciplinary field. She decided that teachers should practice different methods together for meaningful learning, and that such eclecticism would be more profitable in the classroom. The teacher's input in terms of personal experiences and characteristics are a necessary component of successful teaching as lived experiences make the material meaningful for the student.

Esra forgot to mention Literature as an instructional tool, she notices. She believes in the usefulness of literature in language teaching but prefers using literature for homework as well as occasional classroom applications. Esra furthermore accepts the critiques she received from her peers on the 'Evaluation' part of her curriculum map. With more reflection, she would write 'Feedback' instead of 'Evaluation' as she agrees that it provides a better fit with her general conception of teaching. Esra also examines the other student teacher Seval's concept map and finds that Seval has a deeper account of teaching in general, but she also feels that it not so much open to the characteristic details of the discipline and that Seval could be more specific. Esra appreciates Seval's curriculum view for classifying learner types such as visual, auditory and kinesthetic and taking their characteristics into account.

This point in particular brings Esra to reconceptualize her own approach to concept mapping. Now, she would prefer not to express the Teacher and Learner characteristics under the title Theory of language teaching. As a result, viewing the maps of her peers helps Esra reframe her own knowledge. The first abductive and inductive phases are now replaced by deduction and she examines different rationales. Esra argues that Harun put general titles on his map and that he should have opened such generic conceptual boxes and refined their distinctive characteristics to look for their instructional (didactic) implications in the discipline itself.

Identification: Esra admits she needs some brainstorming to engage more in what English Language Teaching studies represent and make her curriculum more meaningful. She wants to attend conferences to see samples of processed curriculum knowledge. Feedback inspired Esra to reflect on the concepts of the discipline. She felt she could better classify the teachers according to types of professional experiences. She did not integrate language politics in her concept map. When it came to be discussed with the students she concluded that each curriculum map demonstrates a personal teaching philosophy. Each map depicts the discipline in various ways, and their approaches indicate their own politics of education. The distinctive point in her map is the role of history in constructing the field of knowledge. According to her, Harun should have put more subtitles and have clarified the instructional topics, as he talks about only two methods grammar translation and communicative approach and needs to account for many more aspects of language teaching. Nevertheless, she appreciates his map's cultural viewpoint, as he reflects about English culture from a global perspective.

Prediction: Courses are not sufficient to acquire professionalism; Esra needs to experience more language teaching practices. She also needs to revisit her lesson plans as regards the historical background of the discipline, and get a better sense of its worldwide potential value for the future. Esra uses Richards & Rodgers' book in her discussion of methods. She thinks teachers should add their own experiences to the methods to improve teaching. They should note their personal traits to make the best out of it and create a coherent, professional profile. Esra gives herself as an example: she sometimes becomes impatient, which may affect her professionalism. She evaluates the learners according to what they bring into the classroom, not as a measure of their learning aptitudes. In the classroom environment, the teacher should notice the students' background, their developmental characteristics, interests, and discover their talents. Commenting on her map, she mentions that linguistics includes semantics and syntax, so you do not need to show them separately.

Model building: Esra's concept map is based on theories more than practices. She considers the national curriculum and knowledge she received during teacher training, which indicates the key role of teacher education in shaping the curriculum values that will be enacted in the classroom. Esra divides the domain of 'ELT' into two main topics, 'Teaching' and 'Language'. Then she divides 'Language' into two sections: 'English' and 'Linguistics'.

She makes two groups of language skills: receptive (reading, listening) and productive (speaking, writing). She classifies the methods under the 'History of language teaching'. She remarks that Harun added something more distinctive besides the categories they studied at the university: a different interpretation of disciplinary knowledge can be noticed on his map. She feels that because he built an original model, this helps her re-think her own positioning.

If we compare the maps of Esra and Harun, both use previous curriculum knowledge constructed during teacher education at the university. Prior knowledge provides the hunch to start the reflective process but, while deliberating about the field of knowledge, the student teachers increase their capacity to work on curriculum at a metasemiotic level. Esra emphasizes the teaching and learning aspects that are key to the transition from theory to practice. Her approach is based on neo-constructivism but she follows structural procedures for instruction: first, a valid approach is chosen through needs analysis, then it is applied to the target group because its application can be meaningful.

Finally the results and expectations are evaluated according to the objectives. Esra focuses on the previously modeled structure that she was given during her teacher training, and does not use her capacity to reach a personal, idiosyncratic interpretation on her own. In contrast, Harun's inner dialogue helps him model a sense of globalization along the lines of a 'semiotic of the self' (Petrilli, 2004). Even if Harun's map seems somewhat distant from known designs of the field, he elicits a sociocultural perspective with global implications and connections that indicate a higher level of metasemiosis. His case manifests the metasemiotic process more clearly than the others. First he interrupts routine conceptions of the domain, he suspends his interpretation of English Language Teaching for a while as he reflects, and then deliberates on the imperialist power of English and imposed English language policies, and finally makes original decisions and suggestions in terms of communication, education, economy, and state governance. His metasemiosis involves knowledge reframing and determines his position towards the English language and culture. The process makes him feel the responsibility of his own curriculum knowledge as it relates to professional action. Thus he develops what Petrilli (2004) has named 'semioethics'. Semioethic "is connected with our critical capacity for creative awareness of the other as other, which implies a unique condition of responsibility investing mankind for life in its multiform manifestations, which presupposes the global condition of interrelated and intercorporeal dialogical otherness to which we are all subject as living organisms (Petrilli, 28, p.16).

Discussion

Curriculum mapping was instrumental in helping to activate reflection on the semiotic framing of the field and consequently helping the students construe a sense of professionalism. Mapping curriculum knowledge allowed the participants to inquire into how they perceived, understood, constructed, interpreted, 'enminded' (Tochon, 2000a) and enacted the discipline taught. They created maps of what they would see themselves teaching. At that time they were only starting to grasp the concept of curriculum, in their attempt at the field of their profession at large, and our discussion helped them focus on what actually was and would be happening in the classroom. The feedback on this process shed light on the crucial role of teacher education courses in the shaping of curriculum contents. Curriculum maps support a constructive view of teaching, as it did for Harun.

Raising Awareness of Signs Systems

The study of semiotic features through curriculum mapping raises awareness of the sign systems and its codes. Student teachers give meanings to signs according to codes of which they are not aware. Student teachers who evaluate and interpret their curriculum knowledge reflect on the value of contents and the expressions of knowledge they learned previously. Such an inquiry process makes curriculum learning more meaningful. Student teachers do not acquire subject-matter knowledge as a set of neutral, sanitized concepts, but rather construct their own perception of relevant knowledge through interpretations, dialogues, collaborations, additions and improvements. They also adapt themselves to new knowledge that is reconstructed by their mutual contributions. Constructing their view of the curriculum then becomes a relevance process: Each time, knowledge is added to prior models, students adjust themselves with new interpretations. As this approach is experience-based, the resulting knowledge is experimental and intersubjective, allowing curriculum mapping to provide a framework for teacher development.

In this study, we have analyzed curriculum mapping as a metasemiotic, and potentially trans-semiotic process, which involves multiple layers of negotiation and design. Curricula tend to represent the authority that aims at fixing meanings for society. The shared understanding in Turkish institutions is that meaning construction can evolve in the students' minds but it is supposed to be stable and normed in the teacher's mind. The teacher gets training to objectify concepts in a way that will permit either their transmission or their reflective reconstruction. Bourdieu (2001) might note that such naturalizing is part of the idea of programming someone else's knowledge and of the school enforcement of the sociocultural and political heritage.

Knowledge is More than Information

As this study demonstrates, knowledge is certainly more than information processing. Its selection and processing emerges from identity processes. *Harun*, for example, has a socio-political view of the discipline taught that differs drastically from the ones of its peers. When he compared his map to theirs, he realized that he missed some methodological dimensions that would be relevant compared to his initial vision. After discussion with his peers, however, he agreed to complement his political philosophy with other stands that indicate that he agreed to change in order to follow external suggestions. Over time the modeling process proves transformative for Harun as he feels an increased identification with his curricular stands.

Esra deeply reflects on language status and how people perceive and create social valorization of particular language practices. She realizes that the current status of English might change one day, given how it is closely related with the current economic power of the Anglo-Saxon world, which could partly vanish in one or two decades. Esra develops a better understanding that her discipline of choice is a matter of epistemic and social representation.

Then while considering Harun's map, Esra sees that Harun has a global perspective on the English culture that shows up on his map, which leads her to revisit her own map. This interaction with Harun's conceptualization of history leads her to reframe her perspective in a way that differs from the orientation provided in method courses, but it is a better fit with her new sense of what is important in what she will do as an English teacher. Obviously it will be an ongoing semiosis as they will begin to teach and continue in their profession. Through the trans-semiosis of these student teachers, it becomes obvious that curriculum is related to shared experience, identities, humaneness as well as conceptualizing and design.

To conclude, curriculum mapping was an aspect of portfolio building. Identical semiotic processes were at work in portfolio building, as in both cases the arguments were linking normative experience. Student teachers' curriculum maps were constituted through the progressive sedimentation of layers of understanding and representation that stimulated semiotic inquiry to frame a personal view of the teaching domain. It urged the students to think deeply about their subject and was very helpful as part of their training.

STUDY 2

Psychosemiotic Analysis of Reflective Conflict in a Video Study Group

François Victor Tochon and Nathan J. Black

EXCERPTS FROM

Tochon, François Victor & Black, Nathan J. (2006). Psychosemiotic Analysis of Reflective Conflict and Equilibrium in a Video Study Group. *International Journal of Applied Semiotics*, 5(1-2), 219-233.

Psychosemiotics—or the semiotics of human cognition—deals with "how humans learn, understand, and use the signs of culture" (Smith, 2001, p.2). It permits an interpretive alliance of the *psyche* and the *episteme* (that is, the way of knowing), of the mind and reason within the social, the cultural and the political, for example in video study groups. This second study conceptualizes professional development through reflective equilibrium. It investigates how conflicts emerging in a video study group setting help preservice teachers both theorize their personal teaching practice and further refine these theories through response to differing peer perspectives.

Group politics have a history. Individualized trajectories hide the durability of old schemes, of cultural patterns that are deeply engrained in identities and preconceptions on the discipline taught. In the study of student teachers' interactions—students whose teachings will soon mirror what the cultural enterprise wanted generations to inherit of implicit wisdom and intellectualized, common practices—we will analyze reflective conflicts and cross-individual constructions that permeate conscientization in collaborative learning groups. Peer conversations constitute a worthwhile means to confront prejudices (Gwyn-Paquette & Tochon, 2002). Conflicts are highly symbolic of something else. A symbol is a sign that hides another sign. To understand the hidden signs in the way groups reflect, these psychosemiotic processes are mirrored through *techne*, the instruments of retroactive vision such as videorecording and visual feedback.

Psychosemiotics of Educational Development

Reflective development occurs through reflective conflicts and implies a situated focus on meanings and meaning-making within their socio-cultural environments (Walkerdine, 1982). Reflective conflicts are necessary to professional development. Professional development includes all balanced, reflective changes that occur in mental (belief, emotional) structures, abilities and processes and enhance both situated knowledge and self-regulation in a professional setting. Semiotic tools provide valuable analysis of this learning mechanism. By extension they provide a broad psychocultural context for learning to teach:

> In practical reasoning we determine the truth or validity of a statement in terms of it's correspondence to the rules of a practice whereas in formal reasoning truth is determined in terms of the internal relations of the statement itself. To reflect on the internal relations alone we have to ignore the metaphoric context. (Walkerdine, 1982, p. 138)

Tochon (2003) has developed a concept of situatedness that is both contextual (in spatial and social terms) and biographic (in personal and social terms). It provides a framework for understanding growth through a historic, biographic lens with a semiotic depth. Video pedagogy can be considered a situated method of growth (Tochon, 1999a and 2001). It defines the interactions of dialogical feedback in encounters for reflective practice. Videotaped interactions are screened, discussed and conceptualized with the goal of creating new knowledge and improving action (Goldman, Pea, Barron, & Derry, 2007). Video feedback induces a *semiosis* process. Semiosis is the simultaneous action of a sign, its object, and its interpretant in any meaning-making process. Best practice is induced through retroactive discussion, and constructive semiosis as a meaning-making process. From a semiotic standpoint, it involves personal and sociohistories, interactional politics, situated negotiations of meaning, and reflectivity. Feedback is socially reconstructive. It can lead student teachers to examine their representations vis-à-vis issues of race, gender, lookism[1], linguicism[2] and ableism, for instance.

The Semiotic Affordances of Curriculum Reading

The effects of video feedback--though anxiety provoking--are fundamental for developing the socio-cultural, situated skills necessary to teaching in a classroom setting. Video self-study characterizes a semiotic inquiry into personal worlds, *Umwelt*s or constructed environments, with which the subject interacts and develops cognitive *affordance*. Cunningham (2002) has borrowed the concept of affordance from Gibson's (1979) approach to perception. Gibson's perceptual ecology situates the perceivers as active readers of their information rich environment. Gibson's notion of environment is compatible with the Deely's idea of an *Umwelt* where organism and environment are inseparable and imply each other.

The concept of affordance relates with the creation of meaning from the perception of meaningful 'niches' within a fluid and dynamic Umwelt. It refers to 'the perceived and actual properties of the thing, primarily those fundamental properties that determine just how the thing could possibly be used' (Norman, 1988, p.9). It also integrates the understanding that sign

---

[1] Discrimination through appearance.
[2] Language racism, discrimination for the accent, for bilingualism, etc

meanings are associated with and negotiated within such semiotic niches (Schumann, 2003; Logan & Schumann, 2005; Burgin & Schumann, 2006). 'A situation provides a suitable niche only for those persons who are prepared to meet and use its affordances effectively. Those not properly tuned or prepared will in some way fail to perform effectively in the situation as given' (Snow, 1998, p.107). This leads us to anticipate that student teachers get attuned to curriculum 'niches' through transformative affordances. These niches are locations for knowledge transformation.

To sum up, information pick-up, or environmental reading is characterized by the perception of affordances. In this model, inquiry is "the perception of affordance, a process whereby we come to read the environment as a system of signs" (p.19). Cunningham extended the notion of affordance to the social and cultural aspects of human semiosis, which changes its definition, "away from its realist origin to an interactionist one" (p. 22). Cognitive affordance would be an integrated part of what Jay Lemke (2000) names the *Ecosocial Dynamics,* for which semiotic practices are essential to characterizing the dynamics of the processes which constitute the system through their mutual interdependencies.

Other semiotic tools like actantial analysis (Greimas, 1966) can help student teachers elicit the forces at work in the professional conflicts they live (Tochon, 2002) and will be used in this second study.

How does reflective change take place? Student teachers are challenged in their interpretations and move through reflective conflicts. They were initially happy with their mode of thinking. But its cozy equilibrium is suddenly interrupted when they watch their actions on video and listen to others' feedback however tactful it may be. They become aware of shortcomings they did not suspect. The disequilibrium that arises with dissatisfaction and reflective conflict leads them to adopt a smarter way of thinking that can eliminate the pedagogical shortcomings of the previous mental representations. They regain some emotional and cognitive balance that will in turn be challenged with new experiences and new video feedback from their peers. The research question is: in what ways can these reflective conflicts be psychosemiotically framed to enhance professional development?

Methodology

Study 2 is based on a case study. The participant is a preservice teacher in a cohort of world language student teachers at a large American university. The student teachers, most of them white female Americans but for a couple of male and diverse students, were required to create a videotape of themselves teaching in their classroom, which they would view prior to the group meeting to take notes of their observations. Each participant (1) chose a 6-8 minute segment of the videotape to show fellow cohort members and (2) created a handout to structure discussion. Each class discussion was audiotaped for transcription and analysis. Data collection was based on video-elicited self-reflections (audiotaped comments during video viewing) and video study group sessions (audiorecorded and transcribed verbatim of peer moderated discussions). The audio recordings are analyzed to determine what value statements participants make regarding their teaching or student responses and to identify what underlying processes are revealed, how participants dialogically confront their representations through video-elicited self-reflection, and what conclusions they reach through the reflective conflict.

Data Analysis

Greimas's actantial analysis is used to understand student teacher's reframing in the conflict resolution. For Algirdas Greimas, any stories—including stories of experience— share a common 'grammar'. "Greimas derives his *narrative grammar* from an analysis of fairy tales done in the 1920s by V. Propp (1986), and from Levi-Strauss's commentary on Propp. Propp discovered that all Russian *wondertales* contain the same basic characters and plot. He isolated minimal functions, *actants*, roles performed by characters and "functions," types of incidents that reappear in an unvarying order" (Katilius-Boydstun, 1990, p. 7). The "actants" are the story functions. Since its development three decades ago, however, actantial analysis has moved beyond its original literary context and productively been adopted in a number of fields that analyse such narratives as cultural rituals, daily life events, news, social imaginaries and discourse practices (such as scenarios created by totalitarian regimes –Wang & Roberts, 2005).

Thus Greimas proposed a semiotic reduction of Wladimir Propp's (1986) seven roles and identified narrative syntagms that could be 'performancials' (tasks and struggles); 'contractuals' (establishment or breaking of contracts); or 'disjonctionnals' (departures and arrival – Greimas, 1987). Greimas claimed that any narrative is based upon this grammar of binary oppositions that underlies all narrative themes, actions and character types, which he calls 'actants' (see Figure 3). "The subject is the one who seeks; the object is that which is sought. The sender sends the object and the receiver is its destination. The helper assists the action and the opponent blocks it. He extrapolates from the subject-verb-object sentence structure, proposing a fundamental, underlying 'actantial model' as the basis of story structures" (Chandler, 2003). Indeed this analytical grid is close to Jerome Bruner's (1984) narrative, innate psychological grammar. Bruner demonstrated that the narrative structure with its subject-verb-object structure is "inherent in the praxis of social interaction before it achieves linguistic expression" (p. 77). Thus "logos and praxis are inseparable" (p. 81).

To sum up, Greimas produced a generative grammar in which a finite number of functional themes in binary opposition are juxtaposed with possible roles (subject-object; sender-receiver; helper-opponent). They generate the semiotic structures of any narrative of experience and as such could be used to analyse verbal protocols of student teachers' professional stories. The narrative sequence employs "two actants whose relationship must be either oppositional or its reverse; and on the surface level this relationship will therefore generate fundamental actions of disjunction and conjunction, separation and union, struggle and reconciliation, etc.

Figure 3

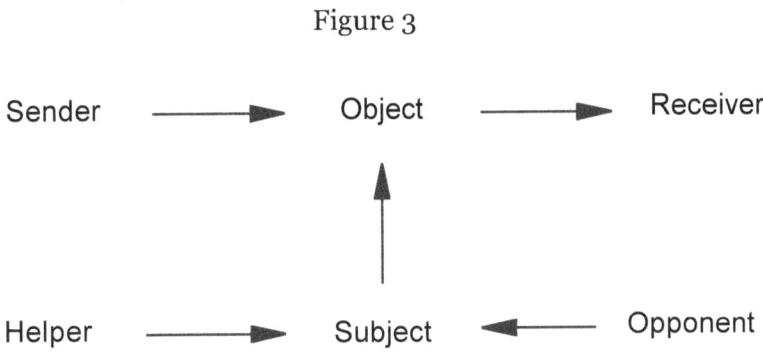

Greimas's Narrative Grammar

The movement from one to the other, involving the transfer on the surface of some entity - a quality, an object - from one actant to the other, constitutes the essence of the narrative" (Hawkes, 1977, p.90). Lenoir (1994) notes that actants are non-human; and, the performance of the actor presupposes competence. Subjects are defined not only as subjects but by the position occupied in a narrative journey, a journey characterized by the acquisition of competences. Actors are constructed as the conjunction of actantial and thematic roles.

Case Analysis

The article is based upon one case study: the case of Carol. She reflects abstractly about students' behaviors and strategies and starts theorizing her practice. In this particular case, she meets a theoretical problem. Indeed she cannot find any congruency between her representations of what her role should be as a teacher, and the very open method her mentor teacher uses. Carol recorded her observations on a digital voice recorder.

The data below come from two stages of this study: (1) the video-elicited self-reflection that she did alone while reviewing the video of her lesson; (2) the video group session that was recorded, transcribed, and then summarized. For lack of space we present selection of the aspects that are relevant to the study.

Video-Elicited Self-Reflection—As Carol watched her video, she recorded a high number of verbal notes, the majority of which resulted from observing student behavior and led her to question her teaching. The themes that arose dealt with student involvement, time management, student resistance to the method, and the efficacy of her method once students bought into the process. The most prominent concern that keeps arising in Carol's commentary is student inattentiveness and unwillingness to participate, followed by continual open ended questioning:

> "First thing I notice and always notice is 5-6 heads down working on the homework. What do you do about this? It hurts me to watch the kids and see so much talking going on. I know they goof off a lot, but it's interesting just to watch them not even pretend to pay attention. It's a very slow five minutes start to class, so I know why some of those kids look bored. My triangle of trouble have been talking for about five minutes now, and it's really interesting to me that I haven't noticed that. That also shows that I really get wrapped up in what I'm doing and aaaaaah. What to do?"

One of the greatest hallmarks of the remarks that Carol makes is the degree to which the videoviewing experience is an honestly self-reflective experience of identifying areas of struggle and trying to identify solutions of how to address them.

Video Study Group Session—When introducing the video Carol asks the cohort's permission to present a technique rather than request feedback. During the 12 minutes that Carol shows video clips, she keeps up a stream of commentary, explaining what she is doing and how it is justified according to theory. Her cohort fellows ask a number of questions seeking further clarification of the theories Carol presents. The frequent amounts of self-critique that appeared as Carol initially viewed the videotape of her teaching have disappeared and Carol's critique is now centered on the method instead. The 20-minute discussion period following the videotape presentation is marked by a much livelier group interaction as a wider range of participants join in. Discussion covers possible ways to adapt the methods she used to traditional contexts, experiences other cohort members share of their attempts to work with it, comparison and contrast with other non-traditional teaching experiences the cohort has had during their student teaching. During this interaction Carol frequently states her misgivings towards using this method, but at the same time advocates a very strict interpretation of the method: "With my seventh graders I get a lot of resistance". To make the point she explained an episode that happened in class involving resistance that wasn't shown on the videotape. A key turning point came as Patricia noticed that some of the methodology being used was similar to a non-traditional experience that the cohort had participated in the previous semester. Cohort members started making evaluative judgments based on experiences or insights gained during their teaching. A reflective conflict arose. This dual increase in both participation as well as evaluative judgments was keyed through a change of reference that allowed the cohort to apply a greater base of situated experience to the discussion at hand.

 Throughout the group session she repeatedly stated that "I'm mixed on the method" and could not bring herself to be either in favor of or being against using the method in her future classes. She reached a reflective conflict climax at some point and had to find a solution. In contrast with Carol, however, other cohort members continually tried to find ways to suggest adaptations of the method to better fit their teaching practices and meet students' learning needs. Carol needed to creatively accommodate theory. Her continual defense of strict methodology seemed incongruent given the degree in which she highly criticized the method at the beginning of the video study group. This focus on methodological consistency in the face of her misgivings reflected the influence of her situated experience upon her understanding. Carol's understanding was tied together with the specific teaching *Umwelt* of her mentor teacher's advocacy of that method, and her attempts to keep a methodologically consistent version demonstrates not only loyalty to his version of the method, but curtailed consideration of other methodological variations while she is working within that system. Thus her conflict resolution had many layers: a personal layer, and a theoretical layer, connected to a third layer of meaning that her students lived in their school lives within their own socio-cultural *Umwelt*. Hence resistance. Students' learning had been forgotten and had to come to the fore. Understanding resistance required for Carol to view (1) homework as extra time to give to school: that is why students were doing it during class; (2) students' ways of pretending and resistance as face, as socially valued; (3) her "triangle of trouble" as the Bermuda disappearance of control and authority through "non-profitable time" and (4) students' talk as socializing, evasion, interpersonal rapport, and intrinsic motivation that could be reinvested. Her reflective conflict resolution followed six phases (Figure 4):

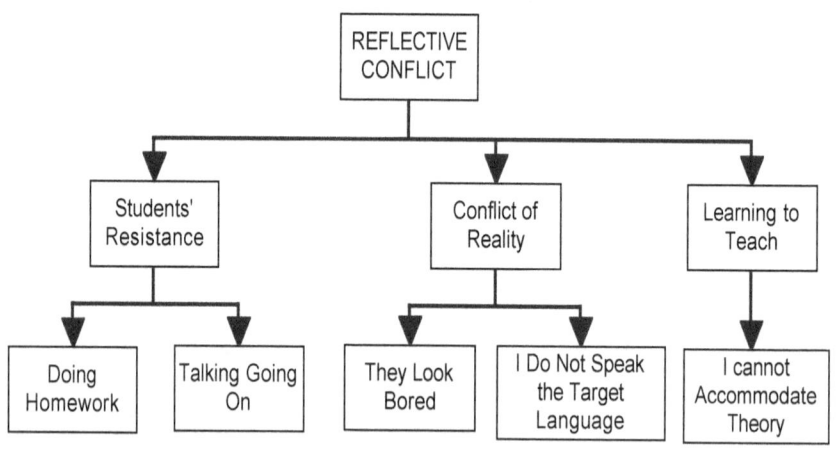

Figure 4
Concept map of Carol's Reflective Conflict

1. Perception of reality conflict

Study 2 - Psychosemiotic Analysis | 59

2. Surprise, being hurt, loosing face

3. Control factor, will at regaining lost mastery

4. Identifying areas of struggle (theory-practice incongruency) and resources (feedback)

5. Unsituating conflict resolution, choosing a more generic mental (theoretical) representation

6. SOLUTION: Creating (conceptual blending) theoretical congruency and refining the specific mental model

Accessing the solution and perceiving *affordance* as a result of her semiotic inquiry would not be possible before Carol would change her representation of the situation. Actantial analysis in Figure 5 illustrates her initial representation. She perceived her mentor teacher--invested with theory and method--as the "Sender". That is, he sent her into a Quest for the Best Practice, Best Practice being the Object of her psychosemiotic Quest for the purpose of Professional Development. During her Quest, Carol perceived that she met a series of Opponents (most of them related with the students and inapplicability of the method/theory) and got Help from her peers. This specifies her reflective conflict.

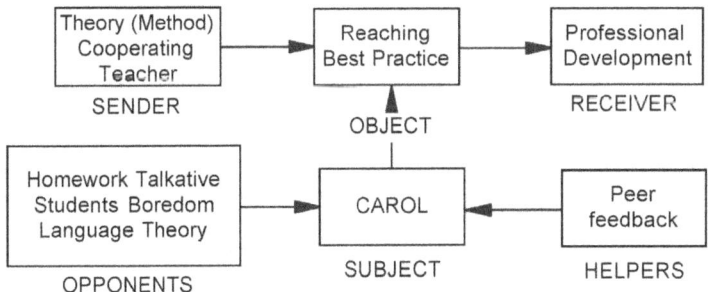

Figure 5
A Greimasian View of Carol's Reflective Conflict

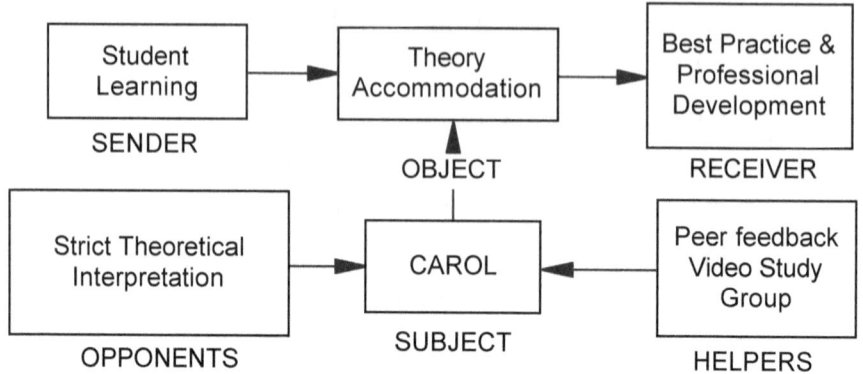

Figure 6
A Conflict Resolution Model for Carol

Carol could not solve this conflict without changing her representation of the Quest and its Agents through reframing. Indeed the conflict was born from the Sender being an Opponent! Thus Carol had to find, through peer discussion, a way to reframe her deficient representation similar to Figure 6. In Figure 6, she can act on the Opponent because it is in herself: the obstacle is HER strict theoretical interpretation of the method. Her goal—the Object of her Quest—should be Theory Accommodation for the purpose of Best Practice. The Sender clearly should be Students' Learning, NOT the mentor teacher or Theory.

Reflective Equilibrium: A Discussion

Reflective equilibrium requires induction and a probability statement about future events (Holland, Holyoak, Nisbett & Thagard, 1989). It relates with Hume's classical analysis of the place of induction in determining empirical truth[3]. The problem of induction is to justify either (a) the generalization of properties of a class of objects based on observations (for example, "All the rabbits that we have seen were black, and therefore all rabbits are black"); or (b) the presupposition that a series of events will occur as it has been the case in the past. Induction in student teaching - as in other fields of life- has very practical implications. All observations may be interpreted as logically implying any probability of future event if the process of induction works. This itself may only be concluded through induction. Predictions issued from patterned events of life presuppose that the culture of events will remain stable. The reliability of induction is always a présupposé, and a hypothesis. There is no rational basis for believing in nature's uniformity and, further, in social life's uniformity. Whether student teachers will make sound inferences from their observations will depend upon both the nature and focus of their observations, and their understanding of the inference process, as leading to conclusions regarding the possibilities of events. What did philosophers have to say about it?

Goodman (1983) analyzed the problem of induction in a new way: he invented a color, 'grue'. Grue mean 'green before time T, and blue on or after time T, where T is a specific future'. Something can be grue if it is green up until a given time, and blue after. Hume's revisited problem of induction became, therefore:

---

[3] David Hume poses the problem of induction in the *Treatise of human nature*, Book I, Part III, section 6, and in *An Inquiry Concerning Human Understanding*, Section IV, Part II.

how can we know, for example, that a spruce is green and not grue? Predictive power is a matter of cognitive economy: confronted with different hypotheses, we tend to choose the simpler one, which has fewer unnecessary assumptions. How does one student teacher know that Joe is chippy and not choppy, when chippy means becoming *intentionally* choppy? Goodman's (1983) response is that inductive reasoning is based on human habit and regularities to which our day to day existence has accustomed us.

Reflective equilibrium serves an important semiotic and psychosocial function. It brings social coherence through the epistemic justification of moral beliefs (Tochon, 2011). Its approach links the cognitive and motivational aspects of the human sense of justice. Reflective equilibrium is not static. It may change as individuals reconceptualize their beliefs and opinions about the issues at hand or reflect on the consequences of certain moral principles. It defines the basis for a realistic and stable psychosocial order that requires up-take by the group members. In this conception, participants have a genuine theory of justice, as Rawls (1999) puts it, whatever their psychosocial positioning. Reflective equilibrium would be the necessary basis for professional *phronesis* (prudence), the neo-Aristotelian way of reflecting on practice that Birmingham (2004) described as the path toward virtue. Humans' affordance to their environment bears a sociocultural and ethical dimension, which would—in Danesi's (2001) terms—position semiotics as the life science that accounts for systems of knowing and confers meaning to hermeneutics and communication. As we will see in the third semiotic study, the actantial analysis can be fluid and dynamic, and it does not need to be based on essentialized constructs.

STUDY 3

Semiotic Grammar of Educational Portfolios: Student Teachers' Struggles in Researching Best Practice

François Victor Tochon and Nathan J. Black

EXCERPTS FROM

Tochon, F. V., & Black, N. J. (2007). Narrative analysis of electronic portfolios: preservice teachers' struggles in researching pedagogically appropriate technology integration. *CALICO Monograph Series* "Preparing and developing technology-proficient L2 teachers", *6, 295-320*.

Electronic portfolios, performance-based standards and reflective activities on teaching experience have come to be viewed as convenient ways of organizing professionalization in teacher education settings. Winsor & Ellefson (1995, p. 3) define the portfolio as a "thoughtful, organized and continuous collection of a variety of authentic products that document a professional or student's progress, goals, efforts, attitudes, pedagogical practices, achievements, talents, interests and development over time". Although web-based portfolios are thus widely used to promote student learning, reflection, and professional development (Stone 1998), very few studies bear on their contents and the way they are organized.

Electronic Portfolios and Quality Teaching

New technologies and portfolios are powerful instruments that can mirror teaching practice and support teacher learning. They enable audio and visual representations of competencies such as presentational and interpersonal skills. They are effective showcases for prospective teachers. They provide evidence through artifacts of suitability for selection in employment before face-to-face interviews are arranged (Dixon, Dixon & Pelliccione, 2005). Evidence in portfolios can furthermore evolve and be updated while experiences improve during the teacher education program, creating a flexible tool for situated reflection. The creative process of building a portfolio is positive for self-confidence regarding the student's professional abilities; actually mapping one's competence is an identity process. Since they target proficiency, creating portfolios represents an effective path towards quality teaching by scaffolding long-term professional development (Barrett, 2002).

As illustrated in Figure 7, "Portfolio construction is a complex social practice with intentions, rules, and standards" (Darling, 2001, p. 107). The evaluation of standards, however, should not be a goal in itself. There is a risk of confusing competence with its performance indicators. Evaluation has to be organized to match other, broader goals with an educational mindset. Depending upon the studies, electronic portfolios have been found to: create a cohesive discourse community that fosters reflective practice (Freidus, 2000); be an excellent tool for attitude change (Winzer, Altieri & Larsson, 2000); help preservice teachers develop their own literacy and stimulate the reflexive approach (Vanhulle, 2002); have a positive impact on learning to teach furthering development as professionals (Hoel & Haugalokken, 2004); allow the identification of cultural scripts and ways of believing that are characteristic of the preservice students' cultural whiteness (Lea, 2004); elicit the values underlying teaching decisions (Sunal, McCormick, Dennis & Shwery, 2005); provide evidence of reflective practice (Orland-Barak, 2005); foster self-confidence in students' professional and technical competencies (Milman, 2005); promote authentic inquiry focused on preservice teacher's self-determination (Harland, 2005); and develop technology skills (Evans, Daniel, Mikovch, Metze & Norman, 2006).

Among these many possible reasons for employing e-portfolios, the most powerful in our opinion is as an organizing tool to help pre-service teachers learn to develop their professional identities through engaging in the narrative reflections that arise through portfolio authoring. One of the major challenges in working with preservice teachers is helping them transition from an academic mindset (in which they work entirely independently and focus primarily on the work of a given semester) to a professional mindset (in which collaborative ventures and growth are vital, as is the ability to develop a holistic vision of their professional development).

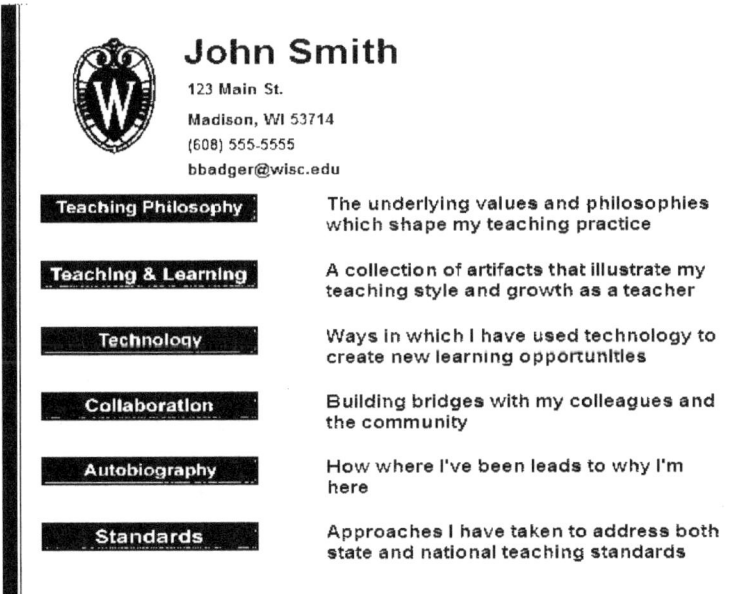

Figure 7
Home Page of the UW Portfolio
(Permission of Education Portfolios & Career Services)

In these arenas, the e-portfolio semiotics is especially valuable, for as the pre-service teachers reflectively describe who they are as teachers to others through their e-portfolio authoring, they also compellingly describe themselves to themselves, thus developing identity and setting the course for their future teaching practice (Holland, Lachicotte, Skinner & Cain,1998; Sfard & Prusak, 2005).

Methodology

To explore and analyze preservice pedagogy, this study analyzes entries from preservice teacher portfolios submitted to address a technology standard and compares cases of struggles, growth and successes as they define, conceptualize and research pedagogically appropriate practices to integrate technology into their K-12 classrooms. Our analytical tool to this end is Greimas's narrative grammar focused on the portfolio entries' discourse that identifies the actors and acting factors of the struggles that preservice teachers faced in technology integration.

Participants

For the purpose of this study, we selected one sample case that contained evidence of the factors at work in preservice teachers' struggles while researching best practice with technology. Best practice was defined according to Fenstermacher and Richardson's (2005) criteria. We reviewed 14 other cases and determined our selection on the basis of criteria such as simplicity, length, variety and the presence of different types of conflicts or critical incidents represented in the portfolios.

Data collection

The empirical data was selected from the electronic portfolio of the preservice teacher under consideration, in which she described lessons she taught involving technology and provided reflective commentary upon such features as lesson design, student responses, and how well their teaching experiences corresponded with School of Education standards. Particular attention has been paid to the ways in which the teachers addressed the School of Education technology standard: *"Teachers appropriately incorporate new and proven technologies into instructional practice. They understand the major social, cultural, and economic issues surrounding their integration"*.

As they author their electronic portfolio entries, all student teachers in the School of Education are taught to organize their narratives according to the following three categories: Context (description of setting and content of lesson), Preservice Teacher Reflections, and Standard Justification (argument as to how the entry addresses a standard). In summarizing and presenting the portfolio narratives, then, we will organize the data according to the same three categories, and thus preserve the structure of the original narratives. In addition, ethnographic observations were made while giving the advanced methods course, supervising student teachers or attending e-portfolio workshops with them. Such observations are used for enriching comments and analyses, and in the Discussion section.

Data Analysis

To analyze the narrative portfolio entries, we use *actantial analysis*, based on a narrative grammar created by Greimas (1976). As we have seen in the second semiotic study, although Greimas's semiotic system was originally developed to analyze literary narratives, it is particularly appropriate for analyzing student teachers' portfolio narratives in that it highlights the conceptual agents that the subjects or participants faced when struggling with best practices. The storied universe can be analyzed in pairs of oppositions interlocked within each plot, which forms a bundle of distinctive functions. Greimas's analysis seeks to find the deep structure of any type of storytelling. It highlights the agents of narrativity in the way they relate to the larger meaning-making process.

Characters may play different functions at different times in a scenario: they may become different actants. "A given character can, for example, serve the function of acting subject or passive object. A narrative action can be said to imply a character who is the sender; a character who serves as the object; and a character that serves as receiver" (Felluga, 2002).

The characters that aid or hinder the quest for the *object* can be either *helpers* or *opponents*, *helps* or *obstacles*. Life stories have their actants too. The actants can be represented by characters or they can be abstract agents like the weather, a computer lab, video or a group of teachers. They play some role in the *subject*'s quest for an *object* that is requested or required by the *sender*, and which will benefit to or serve the goals of the *receiver*. Any actant can "give rise to its opposite: you can have a positive subject in a narrative as well as a 'negative subject' or 'anti-subject' " (Felluga, 2002). A number of modalities can be applied to the model, like the actant's degree of proficiency, simulation or credibility. Regarding classroom situations, for example, the preservice teacher may play the role of a heroine, in the actantial role of *subject*. She accepts a contract that wins her some *helpers* in her struggle against possible *opponents*. These helps or obstacles can be either alive (i.e. characters) or objectal (i.e. material) or abstract (i.e. feelings). The preservice teacher's struggle and quest is resolved when she attains the object of her quest, which can be concrete or abstract, passive or active (as any other story actant). In Greimas's model, the subject will often fulfill a secondary role, as the *receiver* who benefits from the results of the quest. In teaching, the learners may most often benefit and be the *receiver*. In a sense, the plot is a test of the subject's competence. The subject needs to remedy the initial unbalance that precipitated the quest. The *sender* function equates motives, motivation, the impulse or character(s) that pushes the hero character (or subject) to start and win the quest (or object). A sender, then, is any instigator of action that "sends" the hero on the quest. The *receiver* is whoever benefits from the quest: learners, learning, and sometimes the subject is the receiver as well and plays both functions at a deeper level. Any story would organize such deep functional structures; the actantial model takes on a generic format graphically expressed in a flow chart (Fig. 8).

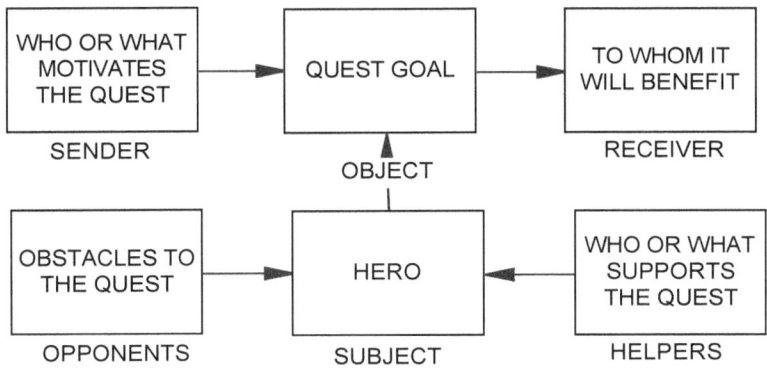

Figure 8
Greimas's Actantial Analysis Details

To sum up and reframe this type of analysis: "Greimas identifies the object as knowledge, and the upper level of the diagram is structurally equivalent to the basic communication situation (sender: message: receiver). The two movements, then, are communication and modification. The story is told, and things change within it" (Katilius-Boydstun, 1990, p. 8). Nevertheless this model is more subtle than first generation communication models. Within this abstract model, actants should NOT be understood as raw and concrete characteristics of people; an opponent can be any obstacle, difficulty, or challenge which hinders the subject of a quest. A character can be a specific actant for a while and then change for another role in the storyline (a process described as actantial syncretism).

Such semiotic tools can contribute to action research, a form of inquiry into the meanings of action that is increasingly used by teachers to improve their instructional skills and promotes a deeper understanding of their teaching practice (Henning, Stone & Kelly, 2008). As a final note, we need to recognize the terminological similarities between Greimasian terms and widely know transmissionist concepts in order to refute any presumed functional similarities. When presented with the terms of *sender*, *object* and *receiver* connected by unidirectional arrows leading from one term to the next, it is natural for readers to overlay a transmissionist perspective on a Greimasian analysis; *sender* and *receiver* are somewhat misleading translations of *destinateur* and *destinataire*. The graphics and comments that we provide in each analysis may help to offset this and demonstrate the complexity and abstractness of the analysis, but it may take unfamiliar readers a few readings through to recalibrate the terms to the Greimasian semiotic system.

Case Analysis: Computer Enabled Assessment

We present excerpts from the participant's electronic portfolio under the categories of *Context* (school and curricular settings), *Reflection* (interpretations, evaluations and observations) and *Justification* (discussion addressing the technology standard). We employ the third person voice during the *Context* summaries in order to reflect the editorial license taken to shorten these sections, but have worked to preserve the original wording as much as possible. The *Reflection* and *Justification* sections, however, contain direct first-person quotes from the portfolios. Although Bee lists a number of technology applications in her portfolio that she has used as a student teacher—autobiographical photographic essays, grading programs, word processing, etc.—the technology she devotes the most discussion time to is Dasher, a computer program that allows her to design her own quizzes. As the Dasher application yielded the richest reflective narrative, our analysis accordingly will focus upon her use of that application.

Bee's narrative is summarized below, while Figure 9 presents Bee's case actantial analysis.

CONTEXT SUMMARY

Spanish II students use the Dasher program to complete a vocabulary quiz that Bee designed. Students could access any school computer during their free time to practice vocabulary and grammar. Students especially enjoyed going to the school Media Center during Study Hall to use the computers and practice Spanish. It allowed Bee to create questions and multiple choices for answers. Students could complete the quizzes on the computer and print off the score with which they are most satisfied. Bee self-labeled her assessment task as authentic, as students used computer technology and typing skills outside of school.

BEE'S REFLECTION

The students love going to the media center to work on the computers. I love to create the assignments for them and just let them work for the hour. The program allows me to create questions and multiple choices for answers. The students are also timed-- they love to test themselves to see who can finish first with the most correct answers. At first, I thought using the computer lab would be hectic and a waste of class time. I was so wrong. Most of the students are on task the whole hour, working on lesson after lesson-- sometimes I let them decide what topic they want to work on and they love that freedom. Moreover, using the computers as an assessment tool is WONDERFUL! I can create a quiz using Dasher, send the whole class down to do the quiz in ten minutes and have them print off the all-ready graded quizzes.

STANDARD JUSTIFICATION

Technology is a wonderful way to organize and present lessons to students in an exciting and engaging way. Incorporating different forms of technology enhances student learning by bringing a larger culture and community into my classroom. Through video, internet, software, powerpoint, and photography, my students can be exposed to and learn about different cultures and communities around the world. Computer technology is a integral part of our students' lives and is a necessary tool for them to master in an ever-growing technological society. The goal for using available technology, then, is to facilitate the learning of the Spanish language through a new and necessary medium.

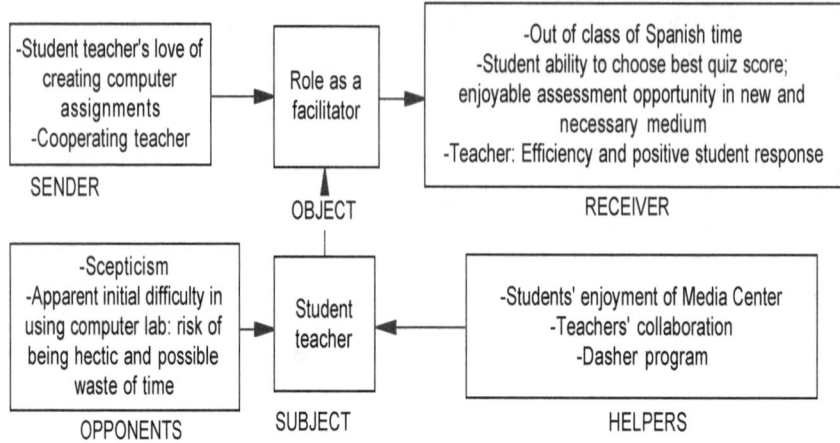

Figure 9
Actantial Analysis of Bee's Case

As shown in Figure 9, Bee's case is more complex in the sense that there are two layers of senders and receivers: considering the actants from the students' or the teacher's perspective. We will come back to this distinction in the Discussion section.

Sender — The preservice teacher's love for creating the computer assignments was not necessarily present at the beginning of this "quest" (her skepticism is noted as an obstacle), but rather something that was developed through interaction. The initial sender that motivated her to initiate her interaction with the computer program despite her skepticism (*opponent*) is not present in her narrative account, and was likely a suggestion from her cooperating teacher. The student's love for going to the Media center was also not initially evident to Bee, but as she saw that reaction (which could initially be classified as a *helper* it became motivating enough to become a *sender* in its own right. Here we are looking at a good case of actantial syncretism, in which the same element shifts actantial roles over time. When Bee professes her love for designing computer programs, the motivation for computer use comes as a result of her students reaction to it. She also does note her love for the program based on its efficiency but that seems narratively secondary to the student reaction.

Helpers — One great enabling factor for this technology use that Bee doesn't explicitly mention is the computer infrastructure of the school: this school has invested in the Dasher software program, and has computer labs that are available for class time. The wireless laptops are clearly helping, but the presence of the actual software itself is just as vital. If Dasher were a Spanish-specific software program, its presence would potentially qualify as a sender, as Bee might be pressured to justify the world language department's investment in such a resource. But as this is not explicitly evident in the narrative account, it should likely be classified as a helper.

Receivers — As with the *sender* category, *receiver* categories likely developed in stages here. The *receiver* category for the teacher is significant (benefits of efficiency and positive student response) because as she overcame skepticism, they turned into *senders* or motivating factors to work with it. In this way the axis of knowledge is self-reinforcing. The benefits go to: (1) Out of class use of Spanish time, a benefit that is shared by both students and preservice teacher; (2) Students ability to choose best quiz score; (3) Students' enjoyable assessment opportunity in "new and necessary medium"; and (4) Efficiency and positive student response that benefits the preservice teacher. Based on their positive experience as *receivers* in the process, Bee's students then became *helpers*, which in turn became significant enough for Bee to have the student enthusiasm be a *sender* for her.

Opponents — Bee perceived two potential obstacles that vanished with more experience: the apparent initial difficult in using computer lab and the risk of being hectic and possible waste of time. As will be detailed in the discussion section, however, the integration of new technologies comes about as Bee is able to address these concerns through pedagogically appropriate means.

Discussion

This discussion can dig more deeply into Bee's case. Our hypothesis is that a deeper level of analysis could account for syncretic senders— senders which influence and transform into other actantial elements—which develop over time, being a hallmark of a mature use of technology. In order to reflect this, it appeared desirable to map some Greimasian actantial analyses— such as Bee's case—onto a more complex concept map than the original flow chart. Greimas's actantial flow chart has always contained the same arrows: the *opponent* arrow and the *helper* arrow directed toward the subject. In this more advanced map, however, the categories would remain the same, but the arrows necessarily take different paths from one narrative to another. If the actants form the basic grammar of any given story, the arrows and varied pathways between the actants manifest the real-world use of that grammar in application. In applying this methodology to Bee's case, figure 10 presents one possible version of how we could visualize this happening.

In Figure 10 straight lines are used to represent the classic paths of influence as conceptualized by Greimas but the dashed and represent interactions between actants over time. In contrast with many of the other portfolio entries reviewed earlier, when Bee wrote up her portfolio entry regarding her use of Dasher, her narrative description focuses more on her process of struggling with technology integration (i.e. the *how*) than on the details of what form the application took (i.e the *what*).

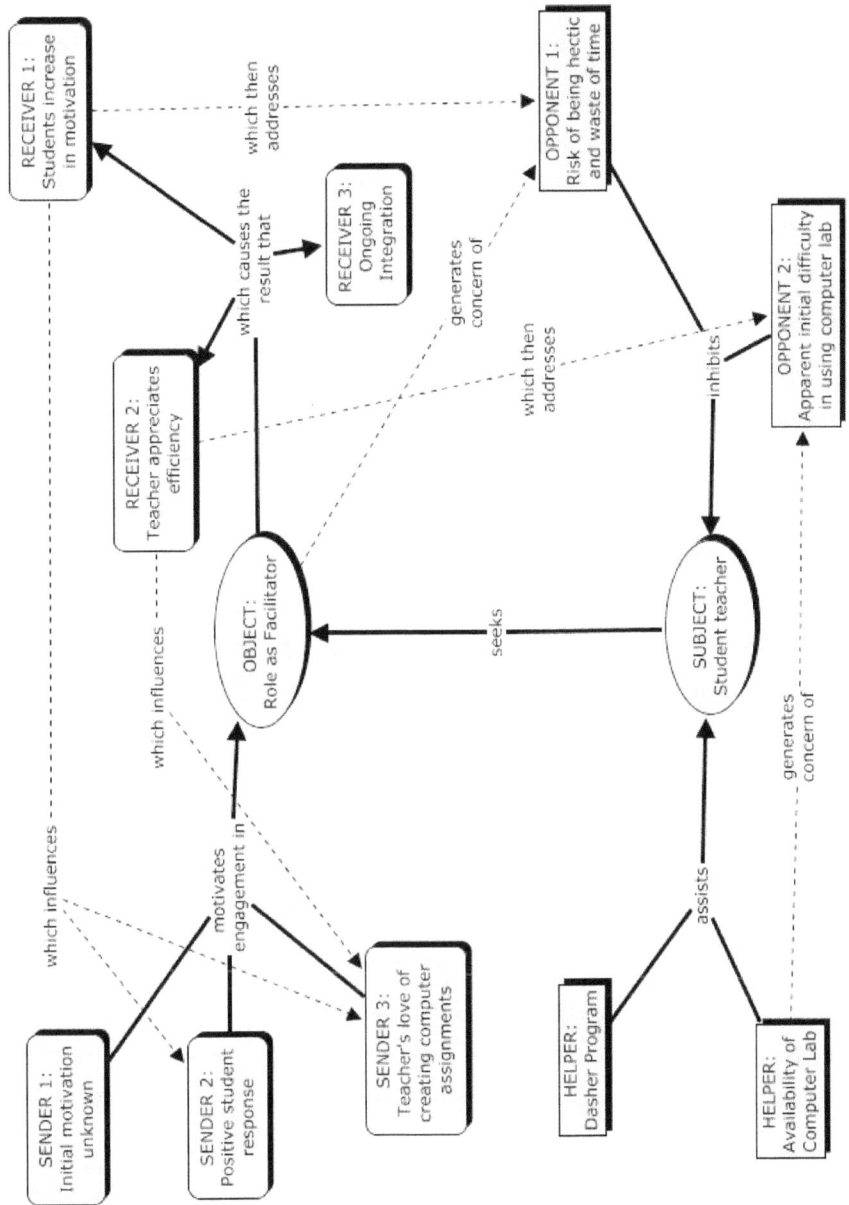

Figure 10
An evolutionary actantial analysis of Bee's case

The concept map above was designed to not only reveal additional relationships between actants in Bee's narrative, but highlight the three fundamental oppositions into which Greimas' system is organized: the axis of desire between the subject and object, the axis of power between the helper and opponent, and the axis of knowledge between the sender and receiver.

The most remarkable aspect of axis of knowledge in Bee's case is the high degree to which several actants are syncretic. As one of the great signs of maturity for preservice teachers is the way to which they adapt to their environments, the degree to which Bee allows elements in the *receiver* actant influence her ongoing experimentation and become in turn *sender* actants—and thereby adjust to the outcomes of her initial teaching—is a significant hallmark of best practice with technology. The additional (not replacement) arrows that are thus added serve the purpose of capturing these evolving plotlines in the narrative. Turning next to the axis of power—the traditional focus for research on technology in education—reveals that the opponents do play the role of binary opposites to the helpers, but not entirely so. Although Bee's concern of difficulty in using the computer lab directly corresponds with the positive fact of its availability, her primary concern is not as predictable, as negative concerns regarding the technical aspects of the positively perceived Dasher program are not present in this narrative. The primary concern is instead derived from a connection with the *object* of Bee's quest, namely that working in the computer lab would prove so unorganized and unwieldy that her primary goal of facilitating student involvement in learning could not be realized. As befits a more complex narrative, then, the *opponents* were not overcome due to continuing emphasis upon the axis of power (such as more efficient scheduling or computer training), but was due to a positive reaction from students—a successful outcome originating from the axis of knowledge. One possible conclusion is that the answers to obstacles in computer use in education aren't necessarily solved by focusing on technology use (the helper) but on other elements in the teaching narrative. Indeed in Bee's case, the object was her role as a facilitator. The perception of potential opponents derived from the identification to this role. This role leads to the smooth integration of new technologies.

One interesting feature of Bee's description comes as she describes her student's involvement with computerized quizzes as "authentic," as this activity is clearly not an emulation of cultural practices by target language speakers. Bee's use of the term "authentic" here refers instead to the social sciences definition of the term which denotes an activity that is a usual practice of the participants—in this case her students' computer usage outside of class. This alternate usage is significant, however, as it underscores how Bee's reflection centers more upon the process of student learning rather than conforming to standards of correctness within field of world language education.

This apparent disregard for a central tenet of communicative language instruction coupled with Bee's apparent fascination with Dasher—a technology whose affordances are more suited to Drill & Kill rather than fostering communicative interaction—perhaps paints a misleading picture of Bee's priorities as a teacher, as our analysis doesn't center on other aspects of her practice presented in her electronic portfolio which are student-centered and creatively integrative with her personal cultural experiences. But this perhaps jarring juxtaposition for world language educators between Bee's heartfelt attention to student learning and her investment in a methodology whose philosophical foundations are skill focused underscores the structural difficulties inherent in technology integration today. Given the time and resources, Bee may well have been able to select a more interactive and communicatively enabling software program than Dasher, but as a student teacher operating under the jurisdiction of her cooperating teacher and within a school that likely has limited technological resource available to its world language departments, Bee had to work with what she had.

One reading of Bee's account might lead an observer to conclude that her success with the Dasher program could lead her to seek out similar programs as an inservice teacher when she is in the position to make such decisions, and this might be true. In looking at the ways in which Bee approached a new technology with robust skepticism and allowed her evaluative opinions to be formed based on student response, however, there is also ample reason to believe that she will continue implement technology into her teaching practice voluntarily and to critically engage each stage of that implementation. Although teacher education programs continually try to influence and shape their students' beliefs regarding what constitutes good pedagogy, both research and experience have consistently shown that this is not always a viable expectation during the limited intervention that is teacher education. If, however, teachers can be encouraged to consistently critically engage their teaching practices and focus on the impact of their teaching upon student learning—as Bee demonstrates—such belief change is much more likely to occur.

Hybridizing the actantial analysis through evolutionary concept mapping brings another, diachronic viewpoint. The visual is obviously more cluttered than the traditional Greimasian one, but it is also more descriptive of the relationships. Another way of doing so would be to differentiate a deeper structure from a more surface structure, or to build two different flow charts: the students' flow chart and the preservice teacher's flow chart. Contrasting the student flow chart with the preservice teacher's flow chart could be an interesting way of making visual the differences in contracts between students and teachers, as the object of the quest would be quite different. Nevertheless moving towards a concept map model offers new opportunities to innovate with the types of links and name them like heuristic schemata do, for example (Tochon, 1990). The arrows' heads would be less immovable. The idea that the influence could go backwards from the receiver to the sender seems very postmodern: recent postcolonial studies emphasized the colonizing influence by the colonizees on the colonizer (Bazna & Mehta-Parekh, 2006). The actantial model has been fixist for 40 years and it might be good to give it some flexibility with superstructural dynamics. Greimas provided a basic conceptual grammar, more complex ones can be created, depending the purpose (Tochon, 1993b).

This might not always be the proper approach to take depending the data and corpus, as portfolio entries have wide variation as to the amounts of detail provided for any given lesson, particularly in the area of time. Bee's narrative, for example, provides a rich amount of description of how she adjusted to student feedback. When mapped out in concept map this way, however, it clearly reveals the amount of environmental response present, as that is one of the areas that is significant from the study. This line of reasoning does not necessarily mean that we are advocating for a redesign of the analysis process as much as it reflects some analysis possibilities; the possibilities of actantial analysis are extensive and place the researcher in discovery mode. To newcomers to actantial analysis we wouldn't advocate blazing new analytical trails unless there were an easily-recognized and easily-realized benefit of doing so.

Conclusion

The way e-portfolios support technology integration has been analyzed and discussed in terms of growing conceptualizations of what is an appropriate practice and what cannot be considered appropriate as regards classroom pedagogy. There is still much to be done, however, to guide the preservice teachers in both the planning and reflective phases. The best teacher education programs are indeed those that interconnect the different activities in the program so that they concur towards a common goal (Clift & Brady, 2005). The discussion of the ways in which the technology uses are integrated into various curricula lies in evaluating to what degree the technology used (the *helper* in most cases) was a good match for the teaching goals (or actantial *objects*). This approach would be in accordance with Windschitl & Sahl's (2002) and Cuban's (2001) observations that technology is an amplifier of specific teacher beliefs. For such an evaluation, we can briefly consider each case separately:

Bee: As her *object* is to work as a facilitator of student interaction, a computerized grammar drill is an odd choice as this normally reinforces decontextualized individual student work. Her pedagogical choice to allow the students to choose the topics under review, however, offsets this and reinforces her teaching goal.

When talking about adapting actantial analysis to this context of analyzing student teaching it is important to note that the Subject needs to be judged based on designing appropriate helps to reach the object. In a literary setting, in most cases the choice of helps are outside of the Subject's sphere of influence—the timely companion, an opportune situation, etc.—making the choice of help out of the Subject's locus of control. In this instance, however, the issue of "appropriateness of fit" between Help and Object is a vital consideration. Teacher education programs should not focus on the available instructional technologies (*helpers*) outside of the immediate context of the teaching objectives (*objects*).

To be pedagogical appropriate, technology integration should match certain principles or criteria that define quality teaching: it should express worthiness and reach broader outcomes than simply technology use. The actantial analyses have demonstrated many principles or criteria that characterize best practice, among which: the subordination of technology to prior pedagogical and curricular goals; the active role of users in such scenarios; the evolutionary adaptation of plans to users, their strategies and styles; the presence of users' integrated evaluations. Bee designed an alternative assessment, which is pedagogically sound. What is most fascinating in the results is the clear tendency of these student teachers to subordinate technology use to pedagogy. In other words technology is not an end in itself: it is clearly a tool that serves others purposes of educational nature.

This addresses a concern present in the literature on technology use. For instance Palacio-Cayetano's et al. (2002)

concern that preservice teachers couldn't conceptualize how technology must be adapted to a classroom context. Meskill et al. (2002) further note the difficulty preservice teachers using technology have in focusing on student learning, adapting activities when technical difficulties arise, empowering students and creating process-oriented learning. The actantial analysis reveals that the struggle and quests of preservices are related with higher educational goals, not technology itself. This is a major result of our actantial analysis: technology is most often a *helper*, not the *object*. This result is crucial. It is confirmed by the other cases in the corpus, not published for lack of space. It indicates the importance of well-scaffolded, pedagogical guidance. The close connection between the different aspects of the teacher education program (methods, student teaching, portfolio elaboration, other educational courses) was probably a decisive factor and, compared to other studies, made a difference.

STUDY 4

When Authentic Experiences Are Framed into Instructional Genres

François Victor Tochon

EXCERPTS FROM

Tochon, F. V. (2000). When Authentic Experiences are "Enminded" into Disciplinary Genres: Crossing Biographic and Situated Knowledge. *Learning and Instruction, 10*, 331-359.

The fourth study applies certain Saussurian concepts to the analysis of learning and instruction. Although Charles S. Peirce and the American semiotic tradition have lately penetrated international educational research—which had long neglected the threefold conception of sign, meaning, and reference now found to conform to neoconstructivist premises—Saussure and the heirs to his intellectual legacy had forged concepts equally compatible with current postmodern trends. In a word, Saussurians are not dinosaurs.

The neoconstructivist conception of education is founded on the assumption that knowledge is constructed within society, that is, pragmatically rather than semantically. In simple terms, semantics is the study of meaning taken out of context, whereas pragmatics is the study of meaning in context. A given word can assume a specific meaning within a specific context, as, for example, the word "dinosaurs" above. Before a new meaning can enter the common lexicon and appear in the dictionary, the community of users of the word must have reached agreement on the context in which this meaning will emerge. It is thus that pragmatic meaning is lexicalised: the value of the meaning is acknowledged; it becomes semantic. A very similar process appears in curriculum and instruction. The learner often attains new knowledge through a metaphorical process. She or he comes to understand through pragmatic approximations and through global indices of similarity. It is only with time that the newly acquired knowledge settles and becomes semanticised. At this stage, it comes to be a part of the pupil's lexicon, her or his inventory of knowledge.

Let me begin by explaining some fundamental Saussurian concepts, which I will be using in the original analysis presented below of curriculum thought, that is, of the instructional design specific to the teaching of a given discipline (in this instance, French). In the Saussurian perspective (Saussure, 1966 [1915]), the linguistic values that govern human interactions are interpreted by indices of similarity and dissimilarity that are grasped along a timeline, sequentially, during the course of interaction—for example, during conversation. What might be called the conversation of pedagogy is equally subject to this rule. At any given moment, the possible meanings of an utterance are examined in terms of differences from and similarities to the utterances that have preceded it, the context, the values associated with specific contexts within a given language, one's personal history (or biography), and a given culture. Saussure makes an analogy between speech and a chess game. The chess game corresponds to a culture that is regulated (every piece has a functional identity), but in which each move, though predetermined to some extent, is made to a certain degree through the exercise of freedom of choice. An individual engaged in speech has the choice at any given moment of organising the sounds of the language and its concepts according to specific combinations of variants. Every term in the language links a sound to a concept. Combinations of terms are linked in linear relationships, and atemporal/associative relationships differentially link the terms used to other terms, or parts of terms, that could potentially have been used.

The classroom teacher is subject to the same phenomenon. She or he experiences the simultaneousness of the two axes of knowledge: an axis along which she or he provides combinatorial coherence between prior knowledge and new knowledge, and another axis which situates the teacher in the immediate present, faced with all the possible associations of the meaning that must be constructed. These two axes replicate the two axes of time articulated in Saussurian theory: the axis of becoming (in a historical sense), which Saussure named diachrony, and the axis of present circumstances, which Saussure named synchrony. As articulated by Saussure, these two axes can serve as powerful analysers of an aspect of the curriculum in thought and action in various disciplines.

In the classroom, for both the teacher and the pupil, over the course of the instructional conversation, there unfolds a becoming of knowledge linked to prior experiences of interactions—what I will call biographic knowledge—and a present-moment relationship to knowledge—what I will call situated knowledge. Biographic knowledge constitutes the pupil's inventory of lexicalised knowledge. Situated knowledge is pragmatic: it occurs simultaneously with experience, at the moment when the learner seeks to capture the meaning of his or her experience. The present moment of interaction intersects with the axis of knowledge linked to prior experience, which is of a biographic nature. Potential associations emerge from this intersection; and it can be postulated that those associations that stand the best chance of being productive in relations with knowledge would be those that "hook into" the learner's experience in learning situations (Tochon, 2000b). These will be perceived as "authentic," because they will engage with the pupil's lived experience.

In the methodology of educational research, the temporal distinction between instructional diachrony and instructional synchrony—in other words, the distinction between the design or the becoming of knowledge and its actualisation through interaction—has led to a distinction between preaction (what preceded interaction); interaction properly so-called, which situates a particular state of the relationship with knowledge; and postaction (what immediately follows interaction). Since it is impossible to interrogate either teacher or pupil about her or his relationship with knowledge in the course of the interaction, preactive and postactive interviews (postactive consisting of immediately retrospective interviews) serve as the methods of choice for investigations into a teacher's or pupil's relationship with knowledge. These two forms of interview allow for an explication of the relationship with knowledge, so that what happens at the intersection of biographic and situated knowledge can be examined. Such explication allows for an understanding of knowledge-in-action, to use Schön's terms (Schön, 1996).

Recent poststructuralist thought has broken with Saussurian duality and binarism, a trend that has led many poststructuralist writers to prefer Peirce's semiotic triangle. What such thinking has lost sight of is that, at the intersection of Saussure's two axes (the microdiachronic axis of the combinations produced in the chain of speech and the microsynchronic axis of virtual associations), there occurs a focal junction point. This focal point is poststructural: it transcends the dichotomy of the two axes and leads us into a study of the outer limits where knowledge is conceived, created, and articulated. It is precisely to a study of this focal point that the concept of authentic experience in education, and in teaching in particular, invites us.

The Theoretical Issues

The role of instruction in enhancing content learning while preserving authenticity

The international educational trend called "didactics" seems almost unknown to the English-speaking world, though it constitutes a major movement in many non-English-speaking countries. Research into and the practice of didactics are based on the premise that we can construct a pedagogy for each subject matter taught: a didactics of language, a didactics of mathematics, and so on. This conceptual movement rests upon very different assumptions than the field known as "didactics" in the United States four decades ago. In its current form, didactics emphasises the singularity of each teaching situation and attempts to integrate academic content with theories of education and pedagogy (Tochon, 1999b). Traditionally, specialists and designers of academic curricula have refused to consider pedagogy an object of interest; so many researchers have tried to construct states-of-the-art for specific disciplines and subject matters without recourse to pedagogy (Bertrand & Houssaye, 1999). In contrast, didactic thought matches pedagogical needs and subject-matter knowledge. Each discipline is viewed through the lens of how it should be taught and learned according to its specificity; that is, how pedagogy should be enacted in particular disciplines because of the specific features of the subject matter. For this purpose, classroom interactions are studied in context to see how subject-matter signs and meaning are co-constructed and how the discipline is actualised into a particular pedagogy.

Social constructivism has led many researchers to become interested in situated learning. The assimilation of specific knowledge does not suffice to enable one to act appropriately in a given field of specialisation: movement in the opposite direction is also necessary. That is, the explication of practice leads to the finding of words to explain experience, the raising of experience to awareness, and the intellectual manipulation of experience. In the present study, it will become clear that this debate, which touches on the process of criterion-referencing learning activities, is critical to recent research in the field of disciplinary didactics. The emphasis here is on the "newness" of didactic trends in educational research. The fact is that didactics is a very lively field of research in many countries, and any old-fashioned associations that may cling to the word "didactic" in the English-speaking world should be dismissed.

Educational semiotics is a field of analysis that is especially suited to be hospitable to disciplinary ways of knowing. In fact, didactics may be defined as the study of how signs are made meaningful in specific disciplines. A content-oriented way of seeing classroom interactions may shed new light on unsolved curriculum issues in the construction of school meaning. At a time when many educators are seriously considering the advantages of the content-centred Japanese model of education, it seems crucial to invoke a compatibilist perspective. Now that we know that a key characteristic of expertise is specific content knowledge (Ericsson & Smith, 1991; Tochon, 1993a), we should emphasise the value of domain-related approaches to learning. In the didactic perspective, content-knowledge education is studied in terms of its necessary transformations within teacher-learner relationships.

It is customary to conceive of curriculum instruction in terms of two opposing approaches: the encyclopaedic approach, which yields a well-stocked mind, and the approach of significant human interaction, which yields a well-developed mind (Pinard, Reynolds, Slattery, & Taubman, 1995; Wraga, 1999). The interest of the didactic model resides in its integrating these two approaches. It rests upon a semiotic triangle with deep cultural implications. Under the didactic model, the constructive, cultural transformation of knowledge emphasised in research on teaching and learning (Shulman, 1990) is analysed in terms of a relational triangle linking learner, subject-matter, and teacher through diverse processes of transformation. Schooling as well as classroom intercourse are analysed within the relational possibilities of three moving loci: the teacher, the subject-matter, and the learner. Researchers working on the relationship between the German tradition of *Didaktik* and current curriculum research into classroom processes, for instance, Westbury, Doyle, & Künzli, (1993), find that *Didaktik*-based research on classroom processes is "the focus of much of the most exciting recent research on curriculum, teaching, and teacher education" (p. 1). They note that content has become an inert concept in most educational theory, and they emphasise that, until recently, content was not central to instructional theory (p. 4) and that important issues may be studied at the intersection of content and pedagogy (p. 5). The implications of this tradition and this research perspective for a theory of learning and instruction are promising. This way of thinking about each discipline may enhance the possibilities for practitioners to attune themselves to the crucial task of facilitating learners' access to specific knowledge cultures.

From subject-matter knowledge to actualisation

It should be borne in mind that the notion of authenticity often appears presumptive: one prepares for situations that will promote authenticity; these are actualised in a setting that is usually less than authentic. In a critical article on "the real thing," Terwilliger (1997) showed how dubious one should be about the possibility of designing classroom experience in a way that will be truly representative of performance in the field. The ways of producing authenticity in a school setting are still mysterious. There are indications of communicative authenticity in children's behaviour, but it is not clear that it serves school goals. Thus there is a gap between authentic experience as planned for the classroom and authentic experience as experienced in real life despite the artificial context.

I developed a model (Figure 11) designed to reflect the dimensions of this clash between practice and its scaffolding (Tochon, 1993c). The model rests upon the two axes of didactics and pedagogy. Where the axes meet, the structural limits of Saussurean binarism are transcended. The axes are complementary yet they enable the conceptualisation of fundamentally different mental spaces. The discipline's inner cultural space "enminds" action (if I may coin a term modelled on "embodies"). This content-specific enminding of action operates along the timeline preceding and following the action. Action is but an expression of this inner culture, of the "mind" of the disciplinary understanding of upcoming situations and events in a classroom context.

On this dimension, the disciplinary mind is diachronic: it is historic and follows the inner narrative of the events experienced through different classroom situations. It is on this axis that experience is semanticised, that is, enminded in the particular vocabulary and genres of a particular subject matter. This first axis, one of disciplinary goal-setting, intersects with the second axis, that of the present tense of pedagogy, in which, for instance, inner intentions may be transformed in specific outer actions. This is the axis of pragmatisation, that is, the actualisation of meaning-making experiences (Figure 11).

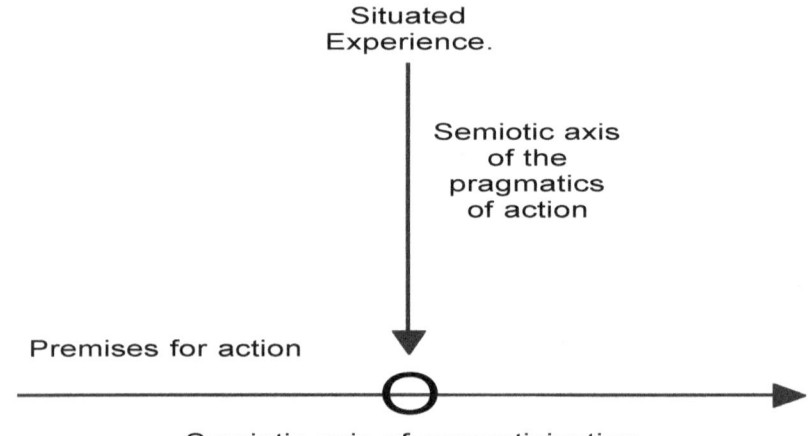

Figure 11
Model of the Authentic Learning Situation

Synchronic (present-tense) interactions move the inner world of the disciplinary culture forward and make it evolve. Thus there is an interconnection between the here and now of pedagogy and the historic mind of a discipline. The disciplinary culture evolves in learners' minds, teachers' minds, schools' inner cultures, and the inner world of research and scientific knowledge.

Certain researchers have referred to this model and proposed time strata valid in specific disciplines (Lacotte & Lenoir, 1999). Gauthier et al. (1997) have shown the merits and the limitations of the model, which should not be reductively interpreted as a clash between "pure" planning and "pure" experience (Tochon & Munby, 1993). At the intersection of the two axes, the inner worlds of didactics and pedagogy merge. A focal break-off point does exist. It represents a different dimension related to the emergence of meaning. One major attraction of the model is that it emphasises this focal point, found at the convergence of two dimensions that intersect, those of school time and space. School time takes on a conceptual dimension, because it is measured in terms of the pacing of contents. Curriculum time situates academic contents diachronically on a horizontal axis along which interactions are lexicalised (put into words) and semanticised (given meaning by being explained). School space, falling on the vertical axis, is interactional. It is experienced synchronically. It constitutes the axis of the pragmatics of action: pragmatics transcend semantics by giving situated meaning to curricular contents. Numerous aspects of the meaning are woven into the situation without all being immediately explicable. Explanation requires time.

Situated experience is found at the intersection of these two axes. It can be partly anticipated by means of the premises that organise contents according to a representation of potential action. But situated experience escapes planning as soon as it begins. We might even postulate that the mind of the discipline anticipates interactions and is incarnated in lived disciplinary experience. This disciplinary experience is reappropriated in order to explicate the mind of the discipline, in order to appropriate this mind itself by checking whether it is truly the expected disciplinary meaning that has been captured, and not some other conceptual element inherent in the situation.

Given the complexity of lived situations, it is normal for experience to exceed the disciplinary framework; but the slow process of explication of disciplinary experience strengthens learning that tends towards the representation corresponding to the mind of the discipline. It is at the junction point of school time and school space that disciplinary experience submerges itself in the mind of the discipline. The duality of the two axes is merely a structuralist relic. Merging them yields a third, poststructuralist model. Focusing research on the break-off point, which is simultaneously a junction point and a boundary line, will elicit the emergence of new ways of conceiving learning, teaching, and school culture.

What constitutes school culture in a particular discipline? School dialogue, discourse, texts and signs, can be considered the fundamentals of school culture in diverse disciplines. We understand them through events that are prototypes or samples of what should be done and learned in typical school situations (Entlewistle, 1995). Schneuwly and Dolz (1997) propose considering the subjects of teaching as *school genres*. They write that disciplinary conceptions are modelled by subject-matter genres: the teacher understands what he or she teaches in his or her discipline through the prototype genres that assemble configurations of subject-matter knowledge. Thus the authors propose analysing the subjects taught within a given discipline as discourses that have been put into words and text as a support to teaching and learning. A genre fills the role of a prototype. Rosch (1973) showed the prototypic function of semantic nodes. It is this function that results in a titmouse being more of a "bird" than a penguin, or a trout being more of a "fish" than a whale. We amass information in groupings based on overall, prototypic similarities. Thus, if learning as such occurs through the recognition of school genres, the explication of these genres is necessary because, being prototypes, they are fuzzy. They emerge from spontaneous practice. The discursive, situational dimension of this practice is lexicalised (put into words) and textualised in textbooks, but never wholly corresponds to them. Thus the approach put forward by Schneuwly and Dolz (1997) is elegant in its simplicity and theoretical economy. It differentiates between the lived language of experience and the textualised wording of that experience for the purpose of communicating it. However, the instructional wording scaffolds an experience that is never fully caught in the words used to conceptualise the experience. At a given break-off point, the words have to become an experience.

The paradox involved here is the same as that of the model presented in Figure 11:

1. One has to *design* disciplinary practice in order to teach it and to scaffold learning; for instance, teaching a child how to describe a prop emerges from a prior conceptualisation of the situation of designing a prop; designing disciplinary practice makes it a genre—that is, a prototype of disciplinary reality.

2. This process of *designing* disciplinary experience relies on the belief that designing/designating authentic experience in words will help provide means for teaching and learning further authentic experiences. However, there is no assurance that the words that designate authentic experience will designate authenticity in classroom communications. If school genres are defined by the *design* of practice, and only school genres can be taught because one cannot access knowledge without prototypical links to reality, it is far from sure that genres can match the experience designed/designated by our words. Why? On one hand, because of the gap between words and experience, planning and actualisation, and on the other hand, because, as this theory affirms, learning is not a matter of words alone.

Terwilliger (1997) stresses that the search for authentic experience "denigrates the importance of knowledge and basic skills as legitimate educational outcomes" (p. 24). It constitutes an elusive, even delusive, quest, because there is no criterion for authenticity. In this regard, Schneuwly and Dolz (1997) infer from the absence of fit between school genres and authentic experiences that we should find further criteria of validity with which to tightly define each school genre. One could define the criteria for each genre of experience more tightly, to find more rigorous ways to look at authenticity (Darling-Hammond, Ancess, & Falk, 1995; Lesh & Lamon, 1992). My own inference is that we will *never* be able to design precise criteria for experiential practice, but we *can* design premises that will scaffold some part of a learning experience, which—because it will be authentic—will escape our own initial wording. These different types of inferences lead research in opposite directions.

On one hand, it is supposed that because experience is not easy to put into words, words have to be refined to the point where they will come close to designing/designating true experience induced by disciplinary scaffolds. On the other hand, it is argued here that criteria will never match the learning experience—and may actually prevent it from occurring; thus the search/research for authentic classroom experience should tend towards the finding of clues to *undefining* events, so that pupils will build their own disciplinary realities. Of course, if one tends in the direction of refining the criteria for school genres, no account will be taken of the risks of actualising them and of possible adjustments when the planned and the experienced intersect. The risks in question emerge when a genre is applied independently of lived circumstances. For example, I witnessed one teacher using the biographical school genre known as the logbook, and involuntarily but systematically teaching children to lie about their experiences by asking them, when she evaluated them, to formulate their feelings in relation to the subject matter taught. Indeed, there are limits to pursuing an investigation in a criterion-based direction: it cannot foresee all the criteria for authentic interaction; and if it did, would it still be authentic? On the other hand, the direction induced from the model I propose neglects the fact that not all authentic experiences will be allowed in a school context. Didactic premises have to be accompanied by ethical rules. There is a break-off point in any conceptualisation one may build; and therefore the study of the intersection between experience and its wording for school purposes may represent one of the most promising paths for new research on ways of building experiences in a specific discipline, using signs and meanings pragmatically, reciprocally, situatedly—rather than as absolutes.

What I am examining here is the potential of this model, taking into account the break-off point between didactic genres specific to oral communication and their authentic acting out. Passage from the semanticisation of a didactic genre to its pragmatisation seems to be revealing of this break-off point in the examples cited in the present study. Pragmatisation refers here to the emergence of meaning in a situated experience, beyond its standardisation.

Following the model of Figure 11, didactics becomes operational at the point where it intersects the other axis, that is, when it is situated pragmatically, in the synchrony of the classroom. Didactic diachrony figures the before and after of learning-interaction in process of becoming, in which what has been forecast dissolves at the moment of exchange. The model explains how it may be possible to plan for didactic intervention and yet have the interaction partially elude semanticisation. Didactic semanticisation is the process used by learners, teachers, and didacticians to explicate and thus standardise teaching and learning within a discipline. In simpler terms, it puts it into words. It leads to the lexicalisation of certain teaching and learning actions and, as Schneuwly and Dolz (1997) write, to defining them as school genres.

The model and the data analysed in this study shed interesting light on the didactic break between the day-to-day and reference practices, a break that may occur on the axis of didactic semanticisation but that cannot exist (as I shall try to show) on the praxeological axis of interaction. Analysis of language experiences in a school context shows that praxis forces transcendence of the practices put in place by semantic tools that represent authentic experience (which have become artefacts by virtue of their being represented). One plans an activity and it suddenly sprouts into something quite different. In a manner of speaking, the pupil must reappropriate the genre via this "other-authentic-thing." The teacher applies words from the school genre to something that is perhaps not very closely related to it. And that's how you wind up with the pupil who went home and told her mother that she was being taught to lie at school. She receives clear indications from the teacher that writing her true thoughts in her journal was a far from welcome action. The genre being taught is not that of a private diary, but rather that of a logbook that one can share with others. It is through the progressive explication of criteria and expectations that one finally comes to learn the desired genre. The "other-authentic-things" learned in class don't appear to be the product of the school genre taught, put into words, and semanticised. Rather, they appear to flow from a social activity defined by the goals and constraints of the situation and of the individuals interacting in it.

To talk of teacher planning and forecasting is to talk of the possibility of stating the premises for the action of learning. The role of premises in making practice explicit has been explored by Fenstermacher (1994) in relation to taking into account the implicit matter that underlies teaching. While Johnson-Laird (1994) has successfully developed the Aristotelian concept of the premise and its role in reasoning, little work has been done on the explicit role of the premises for action in learning. The semantics of action is a topic that is as yet almost unexplored (Richard, 1990). I have worked on the semantics of action, seeking rules for the grammar of teacher actions (Tochon, 1993b).

Here I will attempt a new foray into this field. The school genre constitutes a high-level frame of reference by reason of its actualisation in action. According to the theory of mental models, there exist both models very specific to context and general models. The latter are called "high level" (Holland et al., 1990). The school genre constitutes a high-level model by reason of the variety of its possibilities for actualisation in action. It can be considered a model of situation that underpins the resolution of a wide variety of specific problems (Kintsch & van Dijk, 1988; De Jong & Ferguson-Hessler, 1991; Fayol, 1992). Subject as it is to the context of its actualisation and to individual premises, the situation model that the genre represents is remodelled, be it in the terms of another situation model articulated according to the pupil's premises, or in terms of an "other-authentic-thing," the idiosyncratic practice that we strive to pinpoint afterwards. In this study, I will define experience as the transformation of action that allows for grouping together practices through indices of similarity (Vosdaniou & Ortony, 1989); it relates to attention and not exclusively to language. It constitutes the focal, junction point between the axes of Figure 11.

I will be examining the way pupils put their learning into oral form by looking at possible answers to the following inductive hypotheses:

1. The premises for action that emerge from prior experience model pupils' inner world and thus determine success or failure at the task.

2. Experiential familiarity with the context plays a determining role in the constructive process of learning.

According to this model, the pragmatic links produced with experiential knowledge (whether biographical or situated) constitute the axes of learning and thus explain the importance of oral exchange in learning. If the data confirm this model, they will suggest methodological approaches for scaffolding these authentic experiences.

Methodology

Case study allows for analysis of the axis of the premises for action (the diachrony of learning in a didactic situation) and the axis of the pragmatics of action in the didactic situation itself in order to grasp inductively the viability and verisimilitude of the model proposed in Figure 11. Owing to the available space, this exploratory reflection (on the dimension of *Verstehen*) is modest. Those interested will find other explorations of the topic in Tochon (1996a).

Task description

The learning situation I investigated is one of group learning of oral language skills and communication in French. Different groups were observed during a process of communicative learning that consisted of coming to an agreement to jointly plan and produce a telephone answering machine greeting. The assessment criterion for the task was based on the quality of every pupil's contribution. Everybody had to say one bit of the message. One pupil had the job of showing how the telephone answering machine worked. After that, they divided up the planning and execution of the message. The aim was to jointly create an outgoing message in the vein of: "Hello, you have reached ... please leave ...." A child (the peer), a student teacher in practicum (the novice) and a qualified classroom teacher (the expert), having first learned together how to use a telephone answering machine, were then responsible for regulating one learning group each. The fourth-grade class was divided into three groups.

Participants

The study, which forms part of a larger research program, took place in Quebec, Canada. The level of schooling was elementary, and the children were nine years old. The study involved 459 pupils, distributed in 63 learning groups in 21 classes (the whole results were published in Tochon, 2003), only one excerpt is presented here. Groups consisted of an average of seven pupils. Peer group leaders were chosen by classroom teachers as being positive leaders in the class and capable of regulating a learning group. The student teachers were in third year in a faculty of education (the third year is the last before the degree is conferred). Classroom teachers were qualified "associate teachers," that is, seasoned teachers chosen by the faculty of education, having shown very good ability to supervise practicums over the years and taken relevant training.

Research Methods

In order to examine the role of the premises for action in learning on the diachronic axis, I referred to pupils' preactive and postactive verbalisations. Before or after the activity, pupils explained the premises and preconceptions that influenced them in their learning and how they made their experience explicit or semanticised it. To study the role of context (situation) as the foundation for the didactic pragmatisation of the genre "answering machine message," I relied on activity-observation data supplemented by interviews with the classroom teacher and her student teacher. As we will see, the school genre is reprocessed in the learning situation and creatively metamorphosed into original practice.

Personal interviews with the pupils, the student teacher, and the classroom teacher were organised before and after the task. Verbalisations were recorded and then transcribed verbatim. The whole exercise was the object of ethnographic note-taking. In summary, the analysis relates to what was said by a certain number of pupils before, during, and immediately after the task, with a view to studying how the premises of the experience and then the context of interaction articulated learning.

Authentic experiences in language learning

Experiential knowledge of the context likely plays a determining role in the creative process of learning. The links made by experiences tied to the learning situation probably constitute one of the methods of learning, if the pupil is allowed a certain degree of freedom to explore this context. This influence of the context of the experience is not entirely determined by didactic situations moulded as subjects of instruction. In other words, practice partly eludes instructional intentionality. This constitutes the subject of analysis of the present section: we will examine the links between experience and situation in group learning—and to talk of a learning group is perforce to talk of dialogue and oralisation. Oralisation consists of verbal explication of one's premises or one's action.

The technical term for the conceptual link made between kinds of knowledge is *indexation*. The entry words in the index of a book, for example, point to passages that are linked. Indexation is the foundation of creativity and explains the conceptual links between blocks of information. Indexation is very probably a mode of learning, whence the importance of dialogue about the task in hand. Significant cases of indexation were found that gave rise to change in the work of learning groups in oral language. Before expressing a comprehensive point of view on the events that influenced pupils' knowledge in accomplishing their task, I would like to narrate a few cases encountered in the course of classroom experience.

The first instance of a link between experience and situation took place in a rural school. Here are some indications drawn from my log. It was an early spring morning. I had intended to arrive after the morning recess and had spent fifty minutes driving along a winding road through flat country and past hills where snow was melting in the sun. At last I reached a village and arrived at a school with high ceilings and high windows, and enormous classrooms housing only some fifteen pupils or so. The classroom I was going to faced east; so did the adjoining room, where I was able to talk to the classroom teacher and her student teacher before going to get the pupil who, with them, was going to learn how to operate an answering machine and then regulate a learning group.

At the outset the experience unfolded tranquilly, and I had started recording our observations in the appropriate spaces. For example: "10:50-10:50:30: exploration of answering machine by a child; 11:05: Michael comes to complain of Véronique who is lying stretched out on the table; 11:11: Audrey comes to ask me if I have a hanky." The classroom teacher, having provided some explanations, had done a walkabout, encouraging each child to leave a message and thus promoting individual work. All the other children listened and waited their turn. Just then I noticed that the peer-regulated group was distracted. The weather was beautiful and we were just coming out of a grey period. The children were all grouped near the window and were looking outside. A blue jay was on the tree whose branches came close to touching the great bay windows. The children opened the window slightly and a fresh breeze came into the room. The teacher got up to make an observation but changed her mind. It was the first fine day, and the children's attitude was unaccustomed, intriguing. They were listening to something. Seeing them gathered round the window in the sun was somewhat touching. They were listening to the birds.

The class was silent, and close to the window, the children began to tweet. Then the teacher asked what they were doing. The children explained their plan. One of the pupils knew someone who recorded messages at home with music in the background, and they wanted to record their message with birdsong in the background. The teacher gave them permission to do so. They recorded near the partly open window by bringing the answering machine close to it (see Figure 12).

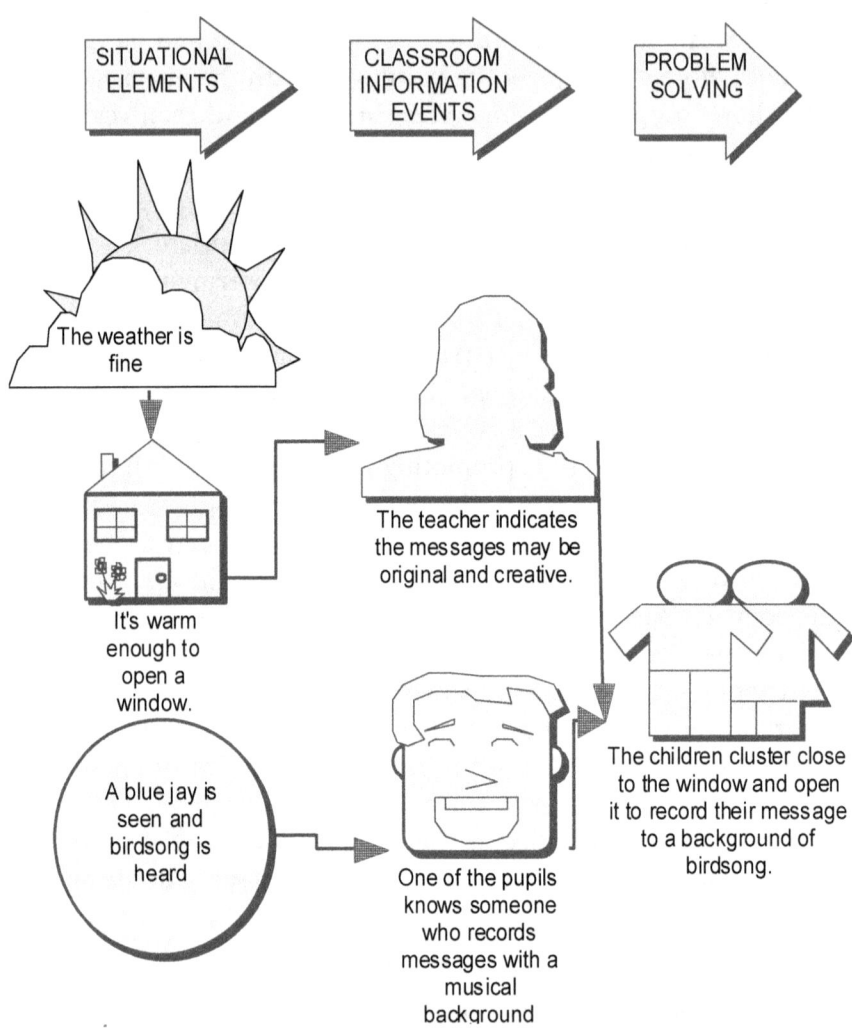

Figure 12
Contextual Links in Learning

The whole of their message was focused on birdsong and springtime. The emotional coloration of their production and the form their learning took was guided by the indices of their immediate setting. The group's learning was not just facilitated by this situation model; this contextual experience, in fact, was integrated into the task and constituted the framework for their efforts. The framework of the work was no different from the framework of their experience. The link made, within the situation, between their task and their setting served as the foundation for their group learning, and very likely as the motivation that led them to creatively accomplish the task asked of them. In this group, the links made between experience and situation in learning formed one of the methods for creating an original message.

We must beware of giving in to the otherworldliness of this description (the flip side of the Bartlett effect). The notes taken by one observer during this research project show that all is not sweetness and light in rural schools in early spring—"10:57-10:59: two kids are making a commotion; 11:17-11:20: three are fighting; 11:21-11:22: generalised confusion." Here, however, is a new index of the importance of the links between situation and task, taken from another class.

The student-teacher-regulated group has decided to focus its message on preparations for Christmas. The date is 6 December. They sing "We Are the World, We Are the Children" then "Santa Claus is Coming to Town," and last, softly, "Frosty the Snowman." The group decides there is too much noise; they have to go to another room. Their objective is focused on Christmas celebrations and fits into the general atmosphere of the school, which has just been decorated. Other classroom activities are also focused on Christmas. "We could do 'Frosty the Snowman,' but the song is too long." The student teacher: "Hello! My little elves and I ..."—the student teacher takes over a large part of the message, after which the pupils introduce themselves one by one and then sing together. One pupil holds down the *OGM rec* button. "That wasn't very good, let's do it over again!" The student teacher: "I'm not going to do the ho-ho-ho again. We have to assign this differently." "We need little bells"—they go to look for little bells— "Where will we have the bells?" "All the way through." They work on fine-tuning their message right till the last minute, and at the end, close their message with "Happy Holidays!" in chorus. What we are witnessing here is a systematic integration of elements of the environment into task accomplishment. Following the session, the student teacher said:

Marielle started it; I don't know whose idea it was. It was one of the pupils saying that we could use Christmas music. They ran with the idea of "Let's have a party" and because it's Christmas time, they wanted to hear music. And as it happened, I had Christmas music on the tape recorder; I went along with their idea.

In a third class as well, the message was indexed to an event that was close in time: since the pupils had previously practised reading and making up jokes, they poured the idea back into their activity. The role played by context is unmistakable. There was a conceptual link on which the activity was built. During postactive reflection on her group's learning interaction, the student teacher mused:

In my group, things started off quietly, because it consisted of two girls and a boy and the boy didn't seem to want to take part in making up a text, a story. I had to take a pretty active role to get things started. But once it did start, it went very well. They had to write their idea down. They had difficulty doing it jointly and sharing. At one point, I told them it would be good for all three to get involved. At last Michel decided to participate in the message, just towards the end. He was prepared to say nothing more than "Hello." The jokes predominated. They had been learning about jokes, so the idea came to them to do something humorous. They took their inspiration from the Garfield comic strip and their joke. At last I suggested they themselves make up something funny, rather than doing a story over again. They ended up finding something by working on the joke and Garfield and all the ideas that came to them. One girl went to look for her joke book. She suggested the jokes in the book, reading them aloud, but I said to them "Does that really tie in with the idea of leaving a message?" I tried to bring it back round to the idea of an answering machine message.

In this situation, what develops is that situational links created by the pupils lead them to leave behind the disciplinary genre presented as the search for an authentic experience; this obliges the student teacher to standardise their creativity, which is then once again dictated by the context (joke book). In spite of everything, both pupils and student teacher are reassured by linking this new activity to one they have already mastered. They thus bring the two activities together, and the links made help produce their zone of proximal development. What remains to be done is to bring together these ideas while finding a way to accommodate divergent suggestions. This orally negotiated locus of agreement ends by defining this group's learning process.

In this instance, as in many others that can't be presented here for lack of space, it would seem that the principle of analogous congruence is fundamental to learning—the principle that invites one to tie together conceptual elements using, for example, a situational image or a metaphor. In general, learning was envisaged as a difference that needed to be overcome in problem-space $A<->B$. If we accept what is currently believed by researchers in the field of creativity, the problem's definition constitutes a significant component of its solution (Runco & Chand, 1995). On this view, the problem-space is defined not by the difference A—B but by the development of a congruence $A<->B$ that will satisfy the transformational requirements of learning and will be in line with a psychosocial disposition of the pupils (De Corte, 1995). Through successive adjustments, the definition models the goal of the task such that it is aligned with more encompassing goals; as the process unfolds, the task criteria are refined and are realised in line with a dual intentionality, one that is both personal and collective. Academic goals are treated as specific instances integrated into personal and social goals and based on information present in the context of the task. The link between knowledge depends on past experience and is constructed using information available in the task setting.

In this section, we have seen that the links between experience and situation subtly underpin learning when pupils are given a certain freedom to model action as they desire. These links can be created with elements from the immediate setting, which corresponds to the co-construction of situation models. Through analogy, indexation contributes to the process of bringing together pieces of information that were distant from each other and thus defines the authentic learning zone.

Beyond disciplinary genres: When learning is othernessing

In language teaching, disciplinary genres represent particular situation models specific to language situations. Since it is no longer possible to think of language didactics as a simple working out of applied linguistics, the language situations studied in class are intertwined with experiences that aim for authenticity. Thus concerns that are both didactic (i.e. disciplinary) and pedagogical flow together and intersect. At this juncture, oral communication plays an essential role. To the extent that language experience is situated in action, the premises for action come up against the proposed genre of action, as part of a situation the pupil may model very differently from the planned didactic model. This is all the more likely if the teacher works from a logic of appropriation and co-construction of knowledge, leaving a part of the experience up to the pupil to decide on.

While one part of action in language didactics may correspond to a frame of reference imposed by the language genre, its integration into practice prompts the emergence of models that exceed the bounds of disciplinary genres: these models the pupil makes his or her own and reinterprets according to the social, mental, and physical context. The demonstration presented in this study has led me to re-examine the concept of "school genre" (*genre scolaire*) put forward by Schneuwly and Dolz (1997), in the light of inductive situation models (Holland, Holyoak, Nisbett, & Wilson, 1990). These models constitute hierarchical structures of situational interpretation that compete with the genres presented, experienced, and thus reinterpreted. Situation models compete with the didactic genre. They may "yield" to the genre, or they may supplant the performance of the genre and produce an "other-authentic-thing" specific to situated practice; such a practice is not exclusively language-based.

On the instructional level, one important implication for the teacher of the model presented is the need to pay much attention to learners' experiential knowledge. As is shown by Figure 13, this experiential knowledge is of two kinds:

1. Biographical: This kind models the premises for action in a learning situation.
2. Situated: This kind is an integral part of the learning situation, even if the teacher hasn't anticipated this beforehand.

The need to take account of experiential, biographical, and situated knowledge involves the teacher in new experiences when it comes to the dialogue with the learner (what has he or she learned in relation to the subject of instruction?). This is equally so as regards organisation of the learning context (learning situation); that is, it is important that the context provided pupils offer a wealth of learning and suit the goals targeted. One can imagine situations with the potential for varying disciplinary instruction (events, objects, posters, directories, resources) which the pupil could use to build knowledge in didactic situations in a manner that was original and not fully prepared for. Certain schools of a new kind have been created on a related principle intended to free up the self-motivated flow of learning (Csikszentmihalyi & Selega-Csikszentmihalyi, 1990). In rich and varied disciplinary contexts, pupils are given a choice among multiple disciplinary stimuli distributed throughout the classroom context and freely assemble their schedules, with the right to decide for themselves on the duration of a learning activity.

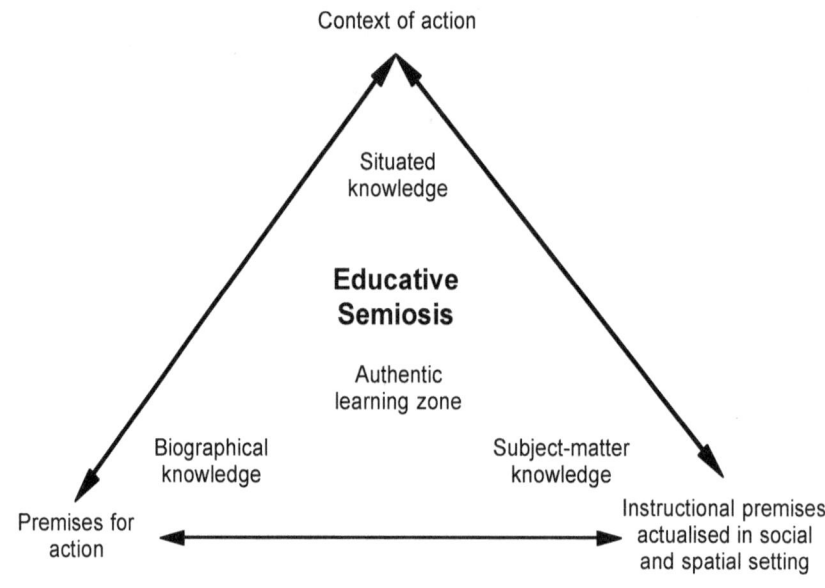

Figure 13
The pupil in the authentic learning situation

In this study I have tried to explore subtle phenomena that are hard to grasp and that influence learning, whatever the methods used to plan those experiences—those experiences that, at a given point, escape a teacher's control because they become authentic. It is not surprising that these experiences are hard to tie into criteria, but they exist nevertheless. Group learning develops freely on the basis of individual premises and the context of the task.

In this fourth study, several linked factors provide convincing confirmation of the importance of experiential knowledge in learning. Indeed, the links made between biographical premises and the context of the experience constitute a mode of group learning in oral communication. Indexation subtly underpins learning by forming links with prior experience, including individual biography and the group's past history, and with relevant indices from the context of the task. Testing of my hypotheses suggests that it is possible to at least partly anticipate authentic experiences if we work on the tension between situations and the premises for action that trigger the pupil's prior knowledge. This could provide a middle way out of the opposition between criterion-referenced performance and communication without referential content. Thus the teacher can present conceptual premises on the basis of which pupils will design their projects.

In Summary

To sum up, this study has suggested the following:

1. The situated knowledge of experience is integrated into the biography of individuals and groups in learning. Group learning is based in part on knowledge available in the task setting. The creation of links between the task and contextualised experience constitutes a method of learning.

2. Analysis of language practices in a school situation suggests that praxis entails going beyond didactic instruments and that an appropriation of the genre as an "other-authentic-thing" takes place simultaneously with the prescribed learning.

3. Seasoned teachers adapt to quasi-authentic situations and admit to disguising their strategies for control (delegation, negotiation, contact, and personalisation of the relationship to teaching), such that activities maintain a natural and spontaneous allure.

The school genres upon which a given discipline rests have a discursive and textual function, but it seems inevitable that they should be exceeded by experience. Better criterion referencing for instructional genres might promote certain academic changes if designed with the goal of ensuring better preliminaries to quasi-authentic experiences in the classroom. Nevertheless, even if the classroom becomes a place for communication and education, it remains hard to plan for open learning. If we want to allow the learner responsibility for a part of the decision-making in his or her learning, it might be better to think of the action of learning in terms of a set of instructional premises that articulate various potential experiences as suits the pupil, so that he or she can appropriate those conceptual elements liable to correspond to an original experience. What is here proposed is that in organising disciplinary activities, teachers act on the two kinds of experiential knowledge integrated into the learning situation: biographic knowledge and situated knowledge. It would thus be up to the pupils to create their learning situation using the various elements presented by the teacher. This aspect is especially important, for example, in deep project-based learning (Tochon, 2013) when multimedia are used for blended learning.

In this study I have presented some proposals emerging from the search for authentic experiences in disciplinary didactics. The disciplines taught in classrooms are culturally bound by very specific types of discourse that shape curricula. They have been defined as didactic genres. These genres characterise the identity and culture of school experience in terms of the premises for specific types of actions. The didactic premises define the social goals assigned to knowledge in disciplinary situations. This feature implies that school genres are closely linked to the politics of knowledge. These disciplinary premises are pragmatic phenomena; they correspond to an intentionality-based orientation. They design knowledge in time; they have a developmental characteristic. They give explicit form to a wording of their disciplines through school genres which can be told and written about. Hence, the genres of the subject-matter taught articulate the premises that posit states of mind, beliefs, and inclinations related to disciplinary knowledge. They are virtual reconstructions of the coherence of knowledge. One feature of school genres is thus eclecticism in search of coherence. In this light, "authentic" learning is in itself a school genre that hides a diversity of experiences and quasi-experiences (experiences of the words that design/designate experiences may produce quasi-experiences).

A perspective is proposed on the role of instructional premises in disciplinary experience. According to this view, authentic experience cannot be fully anticipated, but it can be scaffolded in defining its premises. The perspective is mixed: top-down premises aim at bottom-up experience. On that score, the present proposal respects the situated logic of practice. The perspective of didactics as the enactment of disciplinary genres involves specific features that circumscribe the new field of inquiry within applied semiotics. Similarity-based models emerge from communication experiences in a context of disciplinary teaching and learning. These prototypes or genres enter into a dialogue with situated, genuine experiences. Clusters of features derived from disciplinary genres may be assembled in premises that may provide the basis for genuine disciplinary experiences. This situated model of learning based upon didactic premises could instigate new semiotic research and practice on the ways of enacting instructional models in specific subject-matters.

Conclusion

The Benefits of Semiotic Mapping

The primary finding of the four studies is that semiotic diagrams can be used as training tools for student teachers to improve their professional skills, improve their view of their action or improve their view of the curriculum they will enact in classroom situations. Knowledge mapping proved to be an encouraging semiotic approach which allowed student teachers to get a sense of what was meaningful in the subject-matter as it eased communication between the student teachers and their teacher educator.

Additionally, curriculum mapping facilitated the acquisition of major educational concepts as the maps indicated to students the connections between subjects that they had been taught and those they would choose to teach, thus legitimating their teacher education. Curriculum maps furthermore stimulated reflective practice among student teachers, leading them to re-conceptualize their personal, academic and professional knowledge. The student teachers could then collaboratively discuss the relevance of their priorities, better prepare professionally, and minimize the risks of being inexperienced. In the Peircean view, experimentation is important to fix beliefs. Semiotic diagrams allows the students to review their personal reflections, expectations, past goals and criticisms. The whole process was deep enough that it not only aimed at teaching and learning but gave them a taste for meaningful and deep education (Tochon, 2009 and 2010)

We have analyzed the dynamic emergence of relations between agency and structure, and observed how student teachers reconceptualize their discipline in original ways, including how the structure of their curriculum maps evolves as meanings are never fixed. The way concepts are conveyed in the school context explains why students often fail to personalize what they learned. Student teachers likewise often exhibit this tendency. As this study shows, however, student teachers would like to see knowledge as an effective and functional way of acting in their professional lives. The myth of effectiveness hides the values underlying evaluation. Evaluation is a valuing process and is part of a normalizing semiosis, leading prior knowledge to condition what is considered good education. Reflecting on the designing process helped student teachers understand the fabrication of knowledge for schooling allowing them to become critically reflective.

The student teachers' perception of the curriculum is based on values that differ markedly according to their sociocultural substrate and experiential history. In helping student teachers understand how central the valuing process is to education, semiotic analysis offers a useful interpretive framework, given how the goals of education can in turn be understood as semiotic expressions. When, for example in the first study, student teachers design their curriculum on electronic maps, they tend to reconstruct and reconceptualize their understanding of the subject-matter for teaching. This form of curriculum building constitutes a meaning negotiation endeavor imbued with values that involves political and sociocultural choices, selection, a hierarchizing of values and their enactment into a model that can be taught in schools. Thus curriculum mapping can be an interesting instrument to observe and discuss hunches and values that lead the edification of curriculum choices among postulant practitioners. Viewing curriculum mapping, then, as a process and not as a goal in itself helps explicate how disciplinary knowledge is enmeshed with personal knowledge.

The second study showed that social interactions can be analyzed through a psychosemiotic lense, to verify how the resolution of reflective conflict can lead to professional development. We focused on one case of reflective conflict and analyzed it through a psychosemiotic lense, using a narrative grammar. The data in this second study showed examples that illustrate the process of reflective conflict and progressive equilibrium, with an emphasis on its semiotic framing. In the third study, electronic portfolios document narratives of experience that can be analyzed with the tools of narratology. Like the previous study, we used Greimas's actantial model to analyze the storied universe of world language preservice teachers, this time revealed in their e-portfolios. The integration of new technologies is explored within the perspective of developing pedagogically appropriate technology integration. It addresses concerns expressed in previous studies that preservice teachers could lag behind experienced in-service teachers in conceptualizing how technology must be adapted to a classroom context. The analysis reveals a hugely important conclusion: That technology is a helper, not the object for these preservice teachers. This is a real contribution to the field.

Finally, the fourth study used observation and interview data to verify how authentic experiences may diverge from what has been planned for instruction. The data suggest that academic experience can only be authentic if it is organised on the basis of premises that serve as springboards for conceptual relations that are innovative and thus difficult to set criteria for.

To sum up, when teachers and student teachers try to resolve their doubts, they follow hunches and look for clues, building scenarios and coming up with possible explanations. They sharpen their ability to catch what symptoms are important and need to be trusted, and which ones are irrelevant. Abduction is the beginning of the process of conceptualizing. Ideas are linked by reason and evaluated. It was clear that, as student teachers jointly compared semiotic maps, they also challenged their beliefs, induced genuine doubt and stimulated conceptual reframing. In this process, the student teachers had to fix their beliefs. This implied selective decision-making. Understanding their own abductive reasoning in framing the subject-matter in turn characterized the student teachers' inquiry and gave the whole process an educational dimension. I named that process 'trans-semiosis'.

These four studies, within the narrow area that was explored, illustrated the power of semiotic inquiry for a deeper understanding of education underpinnings. I hope this will inspire other researchers to explore the new, promising field of educational semiotics.

GLOSSARY

Academia: Cultural community of practice engaged in education and research to collaborate in the fixation of beliefs in every branch of learning. The *akademeia* outside Athens was Plato's famous learning center, named gymnasium.

Accuracy: Normed language production.

Code: Semiotic system based on a convention that links a signifier to a specific signified, providing a semantic framework in which signs make sense; when produced in a social context, codes' situated meanings acquire a pragmatic dimension and require an interpretant.

Cognitive mapping (mental mapping, mind mapping, or mental model): Mental processing and structural transformation of information by which a person can code, store, recall, and decode information about the relative locations and attributes of phenomena in a metaphorical spatial environment. Mental models can be mapped and sketched into cognitive maps, scripts, schemata, and frames of reference.

Concept map: Diagram helping to visualize the result of cognitive mapping and indicate the relationships between concepts. Concepts are then connected with labeled arrows, either from the center of the map or in a vertically hierarchical structure. One goal of concept mapping is to elicit knowledge and mental models of individuals, teams and organizations. Another is to capture knowledge from written documents and represent its structure. The addition of resources, such as colors, shapes, files or videos, reports or spreadsheets, to the nodes significantly improves meaningful learning.

Community of practice: Process of social learning occurring when people who have a common interest in some knowledge domain, topic or problem collaborate over an extended period to share plans and projects, look for solutions, and create innovations.

Constructivism: Constructivism views knowledge as being constructed, as it does not reflect any external transcendent reality and is contingent on convention, perception and social experience. As an expansion of social determinism, constructivism assumes that representations of physical reality, including gender and race, are socially constructed.

Constructivist epistemology: A philosophical development that criticizes essentialism in the forms of realism, rationalism, positivism or empiricism. It originated in sociology under the term social constructionism, often used interchangeably. The common thread between various forms of constructivism is that they do not focus on an ontological reality, but on reality construction.

Cooperating teacher: Mentor teacher welcoming a student teacher in his or her class to provide the student teacher with feedback on experimental practice.

Diachrony: evolution of meaning or form over time; historical axis of thought and language.

Discourse: system of representation including a repertoire of concepts and codes for creating and maintaining worldviews within an ontological domain or discursive field.

Encoding: Producing text or discourse in actualizing relevant codes, foregrounding some meanings and backgrounding others.

Feedback: Reporting back or giving information back in a form that can be verbal, written or nonverbal in facial expressions, gestures, behaviors.

Graphic Organizer: Visual aid that helps organize thoughts and ideas (ex: T Charts, Venn Diagram).

Iconic: Meaning-making mode in which the signifier resembles or imitates the signified, as it possesses similar visual qualities.

Indexical: Meaning-making mode in which the signifier is not totally arbitrary but is in some way connected to the signified through similar features.

Instructional scaffolding: The provision of sufficient supports to promote learning when concepts and skills are being first introduced.

Interpretant: Situated meaning that pragmatically emerges from the use of the sign in context.

Interpretive community: Group of people sharing the same codes.

Metalanguage: Language used to describe, analyze or explain another language. Metalanguage includes, for example, grammatical terms.

Metasemiotic: Meta-analysis of semiotic processes, using metasigns or the reference of secondary signs to primary signs. Language education policies, for example, can be metasemiotic, as they regiment linguistic signs through other types of signs.

Methodology: The study and knowledge of methods; term frequently used to designate a set of methods. As an approach to reality, methodology is epistemologically informed and depends upon conceptual frameworks.

Negotiation of meaning: In this process, living organisms or intelligent information systems try to convey information to one another and reach mutual comprehension through restating, clarifying, and confirming information.

Object: Peirce's referent of the sign (what the sign stands for).

Ontology: the branch of metaphysics that deals with the nature of being; the set of entities presupposed by a theory.

Pedagogy: The art and science of teaching children, often used, by extension, for adult education. The term comes from the Greek *paidagogos*, the slave who took little boys to and from school. "Paidia" means 'children', which is why pedagogy is normally meant for children and andragogy is meant for adults. The Latin word for pedagogy, education, is more widely used.

Professionalism: More than simple vocational practice, professionalism characterizes an ethical attitude in professional problem solving, which indicates working with a conscience.

Representamen: Form that the sign takes in Peirce's triadic model of meaning, signifier.

Representation: Textual, discursive, visual, filmic or theatrical construction of reality, reality being the production of systems of representation.

Rhizomatic: rhizomatous: of or relating to a thick horizontal underground stem (called a rhizome) of plants such as the mint and iris whose buds develop new roots and shoots.

Rubric: Set of criteria and standards linked to learning objectives, used to assess students' performance, such as on a test, project, or essay. A type of assessment in which a score is derived from a list of expectations.

Semeiotic or semiotic: Study of signs and sign systems, semiosis and signifying practices at various levels: biology, animal, human, linguistic, with a more philosophical orientation.

Semiosis: Meaning-making process; in Peirce's theory of signs, interaction between an *object*, a *representamen*, and an *interpretant*.

Semioethic: "Connected with our critical capacity for creative awareness of the other as other, (it) implies a unique condition of responsibility investing mankind for life in its multiform manifestations, which presupposes the global condition of interrelated and intercorporeal dialogical otherness to which we are all subject as living organisms (Petrilli, 2008, p.16).

Semiology: Study of signs in the Saussurian tradition, with a textual orientation.

Semiosphere: Whole cultural semiotic space or semiotic ecology in which languages and media interact; concept proposed by the Russian semiotician Yuri Lotman.

Semiotic square: Mapping of key semantic oppositions or binaries in text or practice proposed by Algirdas Greimas.

Semiotic triangle: Charles Peirce's triadic model of the sign including object, representamen and interpretant.

Sign: Meaningful unit standing for something else than itself.

Situated learning: Education that takes place in a setting functionally identical to that where the learning will be applied.

Social context: Environment in which meanings are exchanged. It can be analyzed in terms of the field of discourse, tenor of discourse, and mode of discourse. The field of discourse refers to what is being discussed; the tenor of discourse refers to the participants in the exchange of meaning, including who they are and their relationships with each other (for example, teacher and students); the mode of discourse refers to what part the language is playing with what production channel (writing or speaking).

Story grammar or story map: A story map is a graphic organizer that leads students to discover specific elements from a, written or oral text. It is built upon common elements such as characters and characteristics, place, plot, resolution, and moral or lesson, or a "who, what, when, where, how, and why" format.

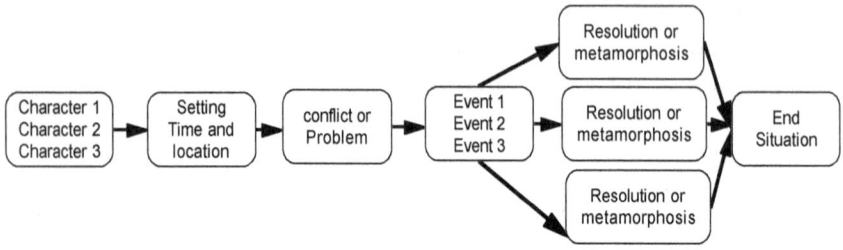

Student teacher: Preservice teacher having initial classroom experiences and practical training under the supervision of a cooperating teacher, or mentor teacher.

Synchrony: *hic et nunc*, here and now frozen at one moment in time.

Trans-semiotic: A trans-semiotic process involves multiple layers of negotiation and design and implies the transfer of semiotic representations through meta-semiosis.

Trans-semiosis is the transformation of knowledge that results from the reframing process of metasemiosis. Since trans-semiosis is so closely related to the dialogical understanding of self and the other—and knowledge is not distinct from the semiosis process—it results that trans-semiosis is an identity process.

Unlimited semiosis: Way in which the signifier is endlessly commutable, functioning in turn as a signifier for a further signified.

REFERENCES

Agamben, G. (2004). *The Open: Man and Animal*. Stanford, CA: Stanford University Press.

Bains, P. (2006). *The primacy of semiosis: An ontology of relations*. Toronto: University of Toronto Press.

Barrett, H. C. (2002). Researching the process and outcomes of electronic portfolio development in a teacher education program. Association for the Development of Computing in Education (AACE). [2006, July]. http://electronicportfolios.org/portfolios/site2002.pdf

Bazna, M. S., & Mehta-Parekh, H. (2006, April). *The packaging of inclusion policy for world consumption : a postcolonial analysis*. Paper presented at the annual meeting of the American Educational Research Association (AERA). San Francisco, CA.

Bertrand, Y., & Houssaye, J. (1999). Pedagogy and didactics: An incestuous relationship. *Instructional Science, 27*(1-2), 33-51.

Birmingham, C. (2004). Phronesis, a model for pedagogical reflection. *Journal of Teacher Education, 55*(4), 313-324.

Bopry, J. (2002). Semiotics, epistemology, and Inquiry. *Teaching & Learning, 17*(1), 5-18.

Bouissac, P. (2011). *Semiotics at the Circus*. New York: Mouton de Gruyter.

Bourdieu, P. (2001). *Langage et pouvoir symbolique* (Language and symbolic power). Paris : Seuil, Essais.

Breault, R.A. (2004). Dissonant Themes in Preservice Portfolio Development. *Teaching and Teacher Education, 20*(8), 847-859.

Brown, D. A. (2002, March). Creative concept mapping. *The Science Teacher*, 69(3), 58-61.

Bruner, J. (1984). *Acts of meaning*. Cambridge, MA: Harvard University Press.

Burgin, M., & Schumann, J. H. (2006). Three levels of the symbolosphere. *Semiotica*, 160 (1-4), 185-202.

Chandler, D. (2003). Semiotics for beginners. Retrieved from: http://www.aber.ac.uk/media/Documents/S4B/sem04.html

Chandler, D. (2007). *Semiotics: The basics* (2nd ed.). New York: Routledge.

Clift, R. T. & Brady, P. (2005). Research on methods courses and field experiences. In M. Cochran-Smith & K. M. Zeichner (Ed.), *Studying Teacher Education: The Report of the AERA Panel on Research and*

Teacher Education (pp. 309-424). Mahwah, NJ: Lawrence Erlbaum & American Educational Research Association.

Cobley, P. (2009). *The Routledge Companion to Semiotics*. New York: Routledge.

Csikszentmihalyi, M., & Selega-Csikszentmihalyi, I. (1990). *Optimal experience: Psychological studies of flow in consciousness*. New York: Cambridge University Press.

Cuban, L. (2001). *Oversold and underused: Computers in the classroom*. Cambridge: Harvard University Press.

Cunningham, D. (1987). Outline of an education semiotic. *The American Journal of Semiotic, 5*(2), 201-216.

Cunningham, D. J. (1998). Cognition as semiosis: The role of inference. *Theory and Psychology, 8*, 827-840.

Cunningham, D. J. (2002). Semiotic inquiry in Education. *Teaching & Learning, 17*(1), 19-24.

Cunningham, D. J., Arici, A., Schreiber, J., & Lee, K. (2002). Navigating the World Wide Web: The role of abductive reasoning. *International Journal of Applied Semiotics, 3* (2), 39-58.

Daley, B. J., Shaw, C. R., Balistrieri, T. Glasenap, K. & Piacentine, L. (January 1999). Concept maps: A strategy to teach and evaluate critical thinking. *Journal of Nursing Education, 38*(1), 42-47.

Danesi, M. (1999). *Of Cigarettes, High Heels, and Other Interesting Things*. New York: St. Martin's Press.

Danesi, M. (2000) *Encyclopedic Dictionary of Semiotics, Media, and Communications*. Toronto: University of Toronto Press.

Danesi, M. (2001). Global semiotics: Thomas A. Sebeok fashions and interconnected view of semiosis. In M. Danesi (Ed.), The invention of global semiotics (pp. 27-50). Ottawa, ON: Legas.

Danesi, M. (2002). *Understanding media semiotics*. London: Arnold.

Danesi, M. (2006). Modeling Systems Theory and the Future of Semiotics. *International Journal of Applied Semiotics, 5*(1-2).

Darling, L. F. (2001). Portfolio as Practice: The Narratives of Emerging Teachers. *Teaching and Teacher Education, 17*(1), 107-21.

Darling-Hammond, L., Ancess, J., & Falk, B. (1995). *Authentic assessment in action: Studies of schools and students at work*. New York: Teachers College Press.

De Corte, E. (1995). Fostering cognitive growth: A perspective from research on mathematics learning and instruction. *Educational Psychologist, 30*(1), 37-46.

Deely, J. (1990). *Basic of Semiotics*. Bloomington, IN: Indiana University Press.

Deely, J. (1994). *The human use of signs or elements of anthroposemiosis*. Lanham, MD: Rowman & Littlefield.

Deely, J. (2007). *Intentionality and Semiotics. A Story of Mutual Fecondation*. London: University of Scranton Press.
Deely, J. (2009). *Purely Objective Reality*. New York: Mouton de Gruyter.
De Jong, T., & Ferguson-Hessler, M. G. M. (1991). Knowledge of problem situations in physics: A comparison of good and poor novice problem solvers. *Learning and Instruction, 1*(4), 289-302.
Denzin, N. K., & Lincoln, Y. S. (2005). The Sage Handbook of Qualitative Research (3rd ed.). Thousand Oaks: Sage Publications.
Dixon, R., Dixon, K., & Pelliccione, L. (2005). The professional electronic portfolio project: The production process. Proceedings of the Australasian Society for Computers in Learning in Tertiary Education. Brisbane, Australia. December 4-7, 2005. http://www.ascilite.org.au/conferences/brisbane05/blogs/proceedings/19_Dixon.pdf [2006, July].
Eco, U. (1990). *The Limits of Interpretation*. Bloomington: Indiana University Press.
Entlewistle, N. (1995). Influences of instructional settings on learning and cognitive development—Findings from European research programs. *Educational Psychologist, 30*(1), 1-3.
Ericsson, K. A., & Smith, J. (1991). *Toward a general theory of expertise: Prospects and limits*. New York: Cambridge University Press.
Evans, S., Daniel, T., Mikovch, A., Metze, L., & Norman, A. (2006). The Use of Technology in Portfolio Assessment of Teacher Education Candidates. *Journal of Technology and Teacher Education, 14*(1), 5-27.
Fayol, M. (1992). Comprendre ce qu'on lit: de l'automatisme au contrôle. In M. Fayol, J.-E. Gombert, P. Lecocq, L. Sprenger-Charolles, & D. Zagar (Eds.), *Psychologie cognitive de la lecture* (pp. 73-105). Paris: Presses Universitaires de France.
Felluga, D. (2002). General Introduction to Narratology. Introductory Guide to Critical Theory. Modules on Greimas: I. On Plotting [July 17, 2002]. Purdue University with support of IHETS/IPSE (the Indiana Higher Education Telecommunication System and the Indiana Partnership for Statewide Education) [accessed July 30, 2006].
http://www.cla.purdue.edu/english/theory/narratology/modules/
Fenstermacher, G. D. (1994). The place of practical argument in the education of teachers. In V. Richardson (Ed.), *Teacher change and the staff development process: A case in reading instruction*. New York: Teachers College Press.
Fenstermacher, G., & Richardson, V. (2005). On making determinations of quality in teaching. *Teachers College Record, 107*(1), 186–213.

Feyerabend, P. (1975/1988) *Against Method*. Revised edn. London, Verso.
Freidus, H. (2000, April). Fostering Reflective Practice: Taking a Look at Context. ERIC Document ED441787.
Gauthier, C. (1997). *Pour une théorie de la pédagogie : Recherches contemporaines sur le savoir enseignant*. Bruxelles: De Boeck Université.
Gibson, J. *(1979)*. The ecological approach to visual perception. *Boston: Houghton Mifflin*.
Gómez, A., Moreno, A., Pazos, J., & Sierra-Alonso, A. (2000). Knowledge maps: An essential technique for conceptualisation. *Data and Knowledge Engineering, 33*(2), 169-190.
Goldman, R., Pea, R., Barron, B., & Derry, S. J. (2007). *Video Research in the Learning Sciences*. Mahwah, NJ: Lawrence Erlbaum.
Goodman, N. (1983). *Fact, Fiction, and Forecast*. 4th ed. Cambridge, MA: Harvard University Press.
Gough, N. (2006). Quality imperialism in higher education: A global empire of the mind? *ACCESS: Critical Perspectives on Communication, Cultural & Policy Studies, 25*(2), 1–15.
Greimas, A. J. (1966). *Sémantique structurale* (Structural semantics) Paris: Larousse.
Greimas, A. J. (1976). *On Meaning: Selected Writings in Semiotic Theory* (Trans. Paul J. Perron and Frank H. Collins). Minneapolis: University of Minnesota Press.
Greimas, A. J. (1987). *On Meaning: Selected Writings in Semiotic Theory* (trans. Paul J Perron & Frank H Collins). London: Frances Pinter.
Gwyn-Paquette, C., & Tochon, F. V. (2002). Reflective Conversations and Feed-back Help Preservice Teachers Learn to Use Cooperative Activities in the Second Language Classroom. *The Modern Language Journal, 86*(2), 204-226.
Habermas, J. (1995). Moral Consciousness And Communicative Action (Trans. C. Lenhardt and S. Weber Nicholsen). Cambridge, MA: The MIT Press.
Hawkes, T. (1977). *Structuralism and Semiotics*. London: Routledge.
Harland, T. (2005). Developing a Portfolio to Promote Authentic Enquiry in Teacher Education. *Teaching in Higher Education, 10*(3), 327-337.
Henning, J., Stone, J.M., & Kelly, J.L. (2008). *Using Action Research to Improve Instruction: An Interactive Guide for Teachers*. New York: Routledge.
Hoel, T. L., & Haugalokken, O. K. (2004). Response Groups as Learning Resources when Working with Portfolios. *Journal of Education for Teaching, 30*(3), 225-241.

Hoffmeyer, J. (2008). An examination into the signs of life and the life of signs. Scranton, PA: Scranton University Press.
Holland, D. C., Lachicotte, W., Skinner, D., & Cain, C. (1998). *Identity and agency in cultural worlds.* Cambridge, Mass.: Harvard University Press.
Holland, J. H., Holyoak, K. J., Nisbett, R. E. & Thagard, P. R. (1989). *Induction: Processes of Inference, Learning, and Discovery.* Cambridge, MA: MIT Press.
Holland, J. H., Holyoak, K. J., Nisbett, R. E., & Thagard, P. R. (1990). *Induction: Processes of inference, learning, and discovery* (2d ed.). Cambridge, MA: MIT Press.
Horrobin, D. (2001, February). Something Rotten at the Core of Science? *Trends in Pharmacological Sciences, 22*(2). Retrieved January 7, 2009 from http://www.whale.to/vaccine/sci.html
Johnson-Laird, D. (1994). *Deduction.* Hillsdale, NJ: Lawrence Erlbaum.
Kankkunen, M. (2004). How to acquire 'The Habit of Changing Habits': The marriage of Charles Peirce's semiotic paradigm and concept mapping. In A. J. Cañas, J. D. Novak & F. M. González (Eds.), *Proceedings of the First Conference on Concept* Mapping. pp. 9. Pamplona, Spain. Retrieved on Mai 2, 2008 from http://cmc.ihmc.us/papers/cmc2004-109.pdf.
Katic E. (2008). *Technology and the Inner Eye.* Saarbrücken, Germany: VDM Verlag Dr. Mueller e.K.
Katilius-Boydstun, M. (1990). The Semiotics of A. J. Greimas. Lituanus, Lithuanian Quarterly *Journal Of Arts And Sciences, 36*(3), 1-13.
Kemmis, S., & McTaggart, R. (2005). Participatory Action Research: Communicative action and the public sphere. In N. Denzin and Y. Lincoln (Eds.), *The Sage Handbook of Qualitative Research* (3rd ed., pp. 559-604). Thousand Oaks, CA: Sage.
Kintsch, W., & van Dijk, T. A. (1988). The role of knowledge in discourse comprehension: A construction-interaction model. *Psychological Review, 95*, 163-182.
Kristeva, J. (1991). *Strangers to Ourselves,* Leon S. Roudiez (Trans.). New York: Columbia University Press.
Lacotte, J., & Lenoir, Y. (1999). Didactics and professional practice in preservice teacher education: A comparison of the situations in France and Quebec. *Instructional Science, 27*(1-2), 165-192.
Lakatos, I. & Musgrave, A. (eds) (1970) *Criticism and the Growth of Knowledge.* Cambridge, UK: Cambridge University Press.
Lakoff, G. (1987). *Women, Fire, and Dangerous Things. What Categories Reveal about the Mind.* Chicago, IL: The University of Chicago Press.
Larsen-Freeman, D. (2012). Complex, dynamic systems: a new transdisciplinary theme for applied linguistics? *Language Teaching, 45*(2), 202-2014.

Lather, Patti (2008). (Post) Feminist Methodology: Getting Lost OR A Scientificity We Can Bear to Learn From. *International Review of Qualitative Research, 1*(1), 55-64.

Lea, V. (2004). The Reflective Cultural Portfolio: Identifying Public Cultural Scripts in the Private Voices of White Student Teachers. *Journal of Teacher Education, 55*(2), 116-127.

Lemke, J. (2000). Across the scales of time: Artifacts, activities, and meanings in ecosocial systems. *Mind, Culture, and Activity, 7*(4), 273-290.

Lenoir, T. (1994). Was that last turn a right turn? The semiotic turn and A.J. Greimas. *Configurations, 2*, 119-136.

Lesh, R., & Lamon, S. (1992). *Assessment of authentic performance in school mathematics.* Washington, DC: AAAS.

Locke, J. (1690). Two Treatises of Government. Book II: An Essay Concerning the True Original, Extent and End of Civil Government. The Second Essay.

Logan, R.K. & Schumann, J.H. (2005). The Symbolosphere, Conceptualization, Language and Neo-Dualism. *Semiotica*, 155-1/4, pp.201-214.

Menand, L. (1997). An introduction to pragmatism. In L. Menand (Ed.), *Pragmatism* (pp.xi-xxxiv). New York: Vintage.

Merrell, F. (2000). *Change through signs of body, mind, and language.* Prospect Heights, IL: Waveland Press.

Meskill, C., Mossop, J., DiAngelo, S., & Pasquale, R. K. (2002). Expert and novice teachers talking technology: Precepts, concepts, and misconcepts. *Language Learning & Technology, 6*(3), 46–57.

Milman, N. B. (2005). Web-Based Digital Teaching Portfolios: Fostering Reflection and Technology Competence in Preservice Teacher Education Students. *Journal of Technology and Teacher Education, 13*(3), 373-396.

Norman, D. A. (1988). *The psychology of everyday things.* New York: Basic Books.

Novak, J. D., & Cañas, A. J. (2008, January). The theory underlying concept maps and how to construct and use them. Technical Report IHMC CmapTools 01-2008. Retrieved on July 2d, 2008 from: http://cmap.ihmc.us/Publications/ResearchPapers/TheoryCmaps

Øhrstrom, P. (1997). C. S. Peirce and the quest for Gamma Graphs. In *Conceptual structures: fullfilling Peirce's dream (Lecture Notes in Artificial Intelligence,* pp.357-370). New York: Springer.

Orland-Barak, L. (2005). Portfolios as Evidence of Reflective Practice: What Remains "Untold". *Educational Research, 47*(1), 25-44.

Palacio-Cayetano, J., Schmier, S., Dexter, S., & Stevens, R. (2002, June). *Experience counts: Comparing inservice and preservice teachers' technology-integration decisions.* Paper presented at the National Educational Computing Conference, San Antonio, TX.

Peirce, C. S. (1931-1958). *The Collected Papers* (C. Hartshorne & P. Weiss (Eds.), Vols.1-6; A. Burks (Ed.), Vols. 7-8). Cambridge, MA: Harvard University Press.

Peirce, C. S. (1867-1893/1992). *The essential Peirce: Selected philosophical writings, vol. 1 (1867-1893)* (N. Houser & C. Kloesel, Eds.). Bloomington, IN: Indiana University Press.

Peirce, C. S. (1877a). The fixation of belief. *Popular Science Monthly, 12*, 1-15. Also in Peirce Edition Project, Writings of Charles S. Peirce, Vol. 3: 1872-1878 (pp.242-256). Retrieved on June 5, 2007 from http://www.peirce.org/writings/p107.html

Peirce, C. S. (1877b/1957). Illustrations of the logic of science. *Popular Science Monthly.* In Peirce Edition Project, *Writings of Charles S. Peirce, Vol. 3: 1872-1878* (pp.242-337). Bloomington, IN: University of Indiana Press.

Peirce, C. S. (1992). *The essential Peirce: Selected philosophical writings, vol. 1 (1867-1893)* (N. Houser & C. Kloesel, Eds.). Bloomington, IN: Indiana University Press.

Petrilli, S. (2004). The responsibility of power and the power of responsibility: From the 'semiotic' to the 'semioethic' animal. In G. Withalmm & J. Wallmannsberger (Eds.), *Macht der Zeichen, Zeichen der Macht. / Signs of Power, Power of Signs.* Essays in Honor of Jeff Bernard (pp.103-119). Wien: INST, www.inst.at.

Petrilli, S. (2008). *Approaches to communication.* Madison, WI: Atwood, Trends in Global Communication Studies.

Petrilli, S., & Ponzio, A. (1998). Signs of research on signs. *Semiotische Berichte. Österreichschen Gesellschaft für Semiotik, 22*(3/4).

Petrilli, S., & Ponzio, A. (2007). The semiotic animal. *Applying biosemiotics: understanding and misunderstanding culture.* Roundtable Organiser: Paul Cobley. 9th World Congress of IASS/AIS Communication: Understanding/Misunderstanding.11-17 June 2007, University of Helsinki, International Semiotics Institute at Imatra. pp.9. Retrieved on Mai 25, 2008 from http://susanpetrilli.com/Papers%20cart/5.Semiotic_Animal.pdf

Pinard, W.F., Reynolds, W.M., Slattery, P., & Taubman, P.M. (1995). *Understanding curriculum.* New York: Peter Lang.

Propp, W. (1986). *Morphology of the folktale* (Ed. Louis A. Wagner, trans. Laurence Scott, 2nd ed.). Austin, TX: University of Texas Press.

Rawls, J. (1999). The Law of Peoples: with "The Idea of Public Reason Revisited." Cambridge, Massachusetts: Harvard University Press.

Richard, J.-F. (1990). *Les activités mentales: Comprendre, raisonner, trouver des solutions.* Paris: Armand Colin, U Psychologie.

Rosch, E. (1973). Natural categories. *Cognitive Psychology, 4*, 328-350.

Runco, M. A., & Chand, I. (1995). Cognition and creativity. *Educational Psychology Review, 7*(3), 243-267.

Saussure, F. de (1966). *Course in general linguistics*. (C. Bally and A. Sechehaye, eds.; trans. of *Cours de linguistique générale* [1915] by W. Baskin.) New York: McGraw-Hill.

Saussure, F. de (1968 [1915]). *Cours de linguistique générale*. Paris: Payot, 1968.

Schneuwly, B., & Dolz, J. (1997). Les genres scolaires. Des pratiques langagières aux objets d'enseignement. *Repères, 15,* 27-40.

Sebeok, T. A. (2001). *Global Semiotics*. Bloomington: Indiana University Press.

Schön, D. A. (1996). La recherche d'une nouvelle épistémologie de la pratique et de ce qu'elle implique pour l'éducation des adultes. In J.-M. Barbier (Ed.), *Savoirs théoriques et savoirs d'action* (pp. 201-222). Paris: Presses Universitaires de France.

Schumann, J. H. (2003, November). *Evolution of the Symbolosphere*. Paper presented at the Great Ideas in social Sciences Lecture, University of California, LA, Center for Governance.

Sfard, A., & Prusak, A. (2005). Telling Identities: In Search of an Analytic Tool for Investigating Learning as a Culturally Shaped Activity. *Educational Researcher, 34*(4), 14-22.

Shank, G. (1992). Educational semiotics: Threat or menace? *Educational Psychology Review, 4,* 195-210.

Shank, G. (1995). Semiotics and qualitative research in Education: the third crossroad. *The Qualitative Report, 2*(3), pp.9. Retrieved on April 4, 2008 from: http://www.nova.edu/ssss/QR/QR2-3/shank.html

Shank, G. (in press). *The Semiotic Inquirer in the Age of Signs*. New York: Mouton de Gruyter.

Shank, G., & Cunningham, D. J. (1996). *Modeling the six modes of Peircean abduction for educational purposes*. Paper presented at the annual meeting of the Midwest AI and Cognitive Science conference, Bloomington, IN.

Short, T. L. (2007). *Peirce's Theory of Signs*. Cambridge, UK: Cambridge University Press.

Shulman, L. S. (1990, April). *The transformation of knowledge: A model of pedagogical reasoning and action*. Paper presented at the annual meeting of the American Educational Research Association (AERA). Boston, MA.

Simpkins, Scott (2001). *Literary Semiotics: A Critical Approach*. New York: Lexington Books.

Smith, H. A. (2001). *Psychosemiotics*. New York: Peter Lang, Semiotics and the Human Sciences vol. 20.

Snow, R. E. (1998) Abilities as aptitudes and achievements in learning situations. In J. J. McArdle and R. W. Woodcock (eds), *Human Cognitive Abilities in Theory and Practice* (pp. 93-112). Mahwah, NJ: Lawrence Erlbaum.

Stanford Encyclopedia of Philosophy (2004). *Feminist Perspectives on the Self.* Retrieved March 8, 2008 from http://plato.stanford.edu/entries/feminism-self/

Stewart, John (1995). *Language as Articulate Contact: Toward A Post-Semiotic Philosophy of Communication.* Albany: State University Press of New York.

Stone, B. (1998) Problems, Pitfalls and Benefits of Portfolios. *Teacher Education Quarterly, 25*(1),105-114.

Sunal, C. S., McCormick, T. S., Dennis, W., & Shwery, C. S. (2005). The Demonstration of Teaching Values in Elementary Pre-Service Teachers' E-Portfolios. *International Journal of Social Education, 20*(1), 81-90.

Terwilliger, J. (1997). Semantics, psychometrics, and assessment reform: A close look at "authentic" assessment. *Educational Researcher, 26*(8), 24-27.

Tochon, F. V. (1990). Heuristic schemata as tools for epistemic analysis of teachers' thinking. *Teaching and Teacher Education, 6*(2), 183-196.

Tochon, F. V. (1993a). *L'enseignant expert* (The Expert Teacher). Paris: Nathan.

Tochon, F. V. (1993b). From Teachers' Thinking to Macrosemantics: Catching Instructional Organizers and Connectors in Language Teaching. *Journal of Structural Learning and Intelligent Systems, 12*(1), 1-22.

Tochon, F. V. (1996a). Grammaires de l'expérience et savoirs-objets : le savoir focal dans la construction de nouveaux modèles de formation. In J.-M. Barbier (Ed.), *Savoirs théoriques et savoirs d'action* (pp. 249-273). Paris: Presses Universitaires de France.

Tochon, F. V. (1996b). Diversités didactiques, cohérence pédagogique (Didactic diversity, pedagogical coherence). In A. Bentolila (Ed.), *L'école, diversités et cohérence* (School, diversity and coherence, pp. 161-176). Les Entretiens Nathan. Paris: Nathan.

Tochon, F. V. (1999a). *Video study groups for education, professional development and change.* Madison, WI: Atwood. Forword by Virginia Richardson and Gary Fenstermacher.

Tochon, F.V. (1999b). Semiotic foundations for building the New Didactics: An introduction to the prototype features of the discipline. *Instructional Science, 27*(1-2), 9-32.

Tochon, F. V. (2000a). When authentic experiences are 'Enminded' into disciplinary genres: Crossing biographic and situated knowledge, *Learning and Instruction, 10*, 331-359.

Tochon, F. V. (2000b). A semiotic theory of supervision as friendship: Cooperative communication as support in second-language education. In S. Simpkins, C. W. Spinks, & J. Deely (Eds.), *Semiotics 1999* (pp. 283- 299). New York: Peter Lang.

Tochon, F. V. (2001). "Education-Research": New Avenues for Digital Video Pedagogy and Feedback in Teacher Education. *International Journal of Applied Semiotics, 2*(1-2), 9-28.

Tochon, F. V. (2002). *Tropics of Teaching: Productivity, Warfare, and Priesthood.* Toronto, ON: University of Toronto Press.

Tochon, F. V. (2003). *L'effet de l'enseignant sur l'apprentissage en groupe* (Teacher's Impact on Group Learning). Paris: Presses Universitaires de France (University Press of France).

Tochon, F. V. (2008). *Globalization, standardization and e-portfolios in teacher education: From organizational learning to social opportunity.* Chicago: Spencer Foundation, 38723.

Tochon, F. V. (2009a). Semiotic Inquiry or the Advent of Deep Methodologies. *International Applied Semiotics Journal*, special issue on "Semiotics and Educational Inquiry". Online journal: http://academicepublishing.com/iasj_special_2009.pdf

Tochon, F. V. (2009b). *The deep approach to Turkish teaching and learning.* Title VI Grant from the U.S. Department of Education. Madison, WI: University of Wisconsin-Madison, Wisconsin Center for Educational Research.

Tochon, F. V. (2010). Deep Education. *Journal for Educators, Teachers and Trainers (JETT), 1,* 1-12. http://www.ugr.es/~jett/articulo.php?id=1

Tochon, F. V. (2011). Deep Education: Assigning a Moral Role to Academic Work. *Educaçao, Sociedade & Culturas (Education, Society and Cultures - University of Porto, Portugal), 33, 17-35.*

Tochon, F. V. (2013). *Help them Learn a Language Deeply ! The Deep Approach to World Languages and Cultures.* Blue Mounds, WI: Deep University Press.

Tochon, François Victor & Black, Nathan J. (2006). Psychosemiotic Analysis of Reflective Conflict and Equilibrium in a Video Study Group. *International Journal of Applied Semiotics, 5*(1-2), 219-233.

Tochon, F. V., & Black, N. J. (2007). Narrative analysis of electronic portfolios: preservice teachers' struggles in researching pedagogically appropriate technology integration. CALICO Monograph Series "Preparing and developing technology-proficient L2 teachers", 6, 295-320.

Tochon, F.V., & Munby, H. (1993). Novice and expert teachers' time epistemology: A wave function from didactics to pedagogy. *Teaching and Teacher Education,* 9(2): 205-218.

Tochon, F. V., & Okten, C. E., (2010). Curriculum mapping and instructional affordances: Sources of transformation for student teachers. *Transnational Curriculum Inquiry,* 7 (1). Retrieved from: http://nitinat.library.ubc.ca/ojs/index.php/tci

Vanhulle, S. (2002, July). How Pre-Service Teachers Develop Their Own Literacy through Personal Portfolios and Peer Interactions. ERIC Document ED470702.
Vosdaniou, S., & Ortony, A. (1989). *Similarity and analogical reasoning.* Cambridge, UK: Cambridge University Press.
Walkerdine, V. (1982). From context to text: a psychosemiotic approach to abstract thought. In M. Beveridge (Ed.), Children thinking through language (pp. 132-146) London: Edward Arnold.
Wallace, R. M. (2004). A framework for understanding teaching with the Internet. *American Educational Research Journal, 41*(2), 447–488.
Wang, Y. (2002). From teacher-centredness to student-centredness: Are preservice teachers making the conceptual shift when teaching in information age classrooms? *Educational Media International, 39*(3–4), 257–265.
Wang, Y. & Roberts, C. W. (2005). Actantial analysis: Greimas's structural approach to the analysis of self-narratives. Narrative Inquiry, *15*(1), 51-74.
Westbury, I., Doyle, W., & Künzli, R. (1993). *The German didactic tradition: Implications for pedagogical research.* Champaign, IL: University of Illinois at Urbana-Champaign.
Windschitl, M., & Sahl, K. (2002). Tracing teachers' use of technology in a laptop computer school: The interplay of teacher beliefs, social dynamics, and institutional culture. *American Educational Research Journal, 39*(1), 165–205.
Winsor, J. T., & Ellefson, B. A. (1995). Professional portfolios in teacher education: An exploration of their value and potential. *The Teacher Educator, 31,* 68-74.
Winzer, M., Altieri, E., & Larsson, V. (2000). Portfolios as a Tool for Attitude Change. *Rural Special Education Quarterly, 19*(3-4), 72-81.
Wraga, W.G. (1999). Extracting sun-beams out of cucumbers: The retreat from practice in reconceptualized curriculum studies. *Educational Researcher, 28*(1): 4-13.
Urban, G. (2006). Metasemiosis and metapragmatics. *Encyclopedia of Language and Linguistics* (2nd Ed. Vol. 8, pp.88-91). London, UK: Elsevier.
Zhao, Y., Pugh, K., Sheldon, S., Byers, J. (2002). Conditions for classroom technology innovations. *Teachers College Record, 104,* 482-515.

DEEP EDUCATION PRESS
SCIENTIFIC BOARD MEMBERS

Dr. Gilles Baillat, Rector, ex-Director of the Conference of Directors of French Teacher Education University Institutes (CDIUFM), University of Reims, France

Dr. Niels Brouwer, Graduate School of Education, Radboud Universiteit Nijmegen, The Netherlands

Dr. Yuangshan Chuang, President of Asia Pacific Association of Multimedia Assisted Language Learning, NETPAW Director, Department of English, Kun Shan University, Taiwan, ROC

Dr. José Correia, Dean, Faculty of Education, University of Porto, Portugal

Dr. Muhammet Demirbilek, Assistant Professor and Head, Educational Science Department, Suleyman Demirel University, Isparta, Turkey

Bertha Du-Babcock, Professor, Department of English for Business, City University of Hong Kong, Hong Kong, China

Marc Durand, Professor, Faculty of Psychology and Education, University of Geneva, Switzerland

Dr. Paul Durning, Emeritus Professor, ex-Head of the Doctoral School, first Director of the French National Observatory (ONED), First vice president of EUSARF. University of Paris X Nanterre, Paris, France

Dr. Stephanie Fonvielle, Associate Professor, Teacher Education University Institute, University of Aix-Marseille, France

Dr. Mingle Gao, Dean, College of Education, Beijing Language and Culture University (BLCU), Beijing, China

Dr. Liliana Morandi, Associate Professor, National University of Rio Cuarto, Cordoba, Argentina

Dr. Joëlle Morrissette, Professor, Department of Educational Psychology, Université of Montreal, Quebec, Canada

Dr. Thi Cuc Phuong Nguyen, Vice Rector, University of Hanoi, Hanoi, Vietnam

Dr. Shirley O'Neill, Associate Professor, President of the International Society for leadership in Pedagogies and Learning, University of Southern Queensland, Queensland Australia

Dr. José-Luis Ortega, Professor, Foreign Language Education, Faculty of Education, University of Granada, Spain

Dr. Surendra Pathak, Head and Professor, Department of Value Education, IASE University of Gandhi Viday Mandir, India

Dr. Shen Qi, Associate Professor, Shanghai Foreign Studies University (SHISU), Shanghai, China

Dr. Timothy Reagan, Professor and Dean of the Graduate School of Education, Nazarbayev University, Kazaksthan

Dr. Antonia Schleicher, Professor, NARLC Director and NCTOLCTL Executive Director, ACTFL Board member, Indiana University-Bloomington, USA

Dr. Kemal Silay, Professor and Director of the Flagship Program, Department of Central Eurasia, Indiana University-Bloomington, USA

Dr. Ronghui Zhao, Director, Institute of Linguistic Studies, Shanghai Foreign Studies University, Shanghai, China

Other referees may be contacted depending the nature and topic of the manuscript proposed.

Contact: publisher@deepeducationpress.org

Author's Biosketch

Francois Victor Tochon, a Professor at the University of Wisconsin-Madison, is heading World Language Education in the Department of Curriculum & Instruction, a Department ranked #1 of its specialty for 15 years in the United States. He has a Ph.D. in Applied Linguistics (Laval), a Ph.D. in Educational Psychology (Ottawa), and has received three Honorary Doctorates from two universities in Argentina and Peru and one international Asia-Pacific association, as well as a Honorary Professorship from Henan University of Technology. With 42 books and more than 250 articles and book chapters to his credit, Professor Tochon has also been Visiting Professor in many universities in 20 countries. He is currently published in 14 languages. He received the 2010 Award of Best Review of Research from the American Educational Research Association. As President of the International Network for Language Education Policy Studies, Prof. Tochon received the 2012 Award of International Research Excellence from the University of Granada, Spain. He is among the 1% most visited profiles of LinkedIn. He is also the designer and Chairman of the Deep Institute, an academic institution that proposes to students to design their own programs and degrees with the help of academic mentors. For the merits of the Deep Approach, Prof. Tochon was awarded the medal of the Council Chairperson of the Lions Club International, and the Quest medal of the Chairperson of the Lions Club International Foundation for Service to Humanity. His 2014 book Help *Them Learn a Language Deeply* became a best seller. His 2015 book *Language Education Policy Unlimited* received the Amazon Distinguished Book Award. International Ambassador for isIPAL in Australia, Prof. Tochon received the 2015 Excellence in Diversity Award from the University of Wisconsin-Madison, the 2015 International Scholar Award of Shanghai Normal University, and 2015 Eminent Scholar Award from the University of Southern Queensland. In 2017, he organized a bi-continental conference on school inclusion and the identities of refugee migrant children, sponsored by the Spencer Foundation, at the University of Wisconsin-Madison and at the University of Paris 3 Sorbonne Nouvelle.

Guide to Authors

What our Publishing Team can offer:

- ➢ An international editorial team, in more than 20 universities around the world.
- ➢ Dedicated and experienced topic editors who will review and provide feedback on your initial proposal.
- ➢ A specific format that will speed up the production of your book and its publication.
- ➢ Higher royalties than most publishers and a discount on batch orders of 25+ copies.
- ➢ Global distribution and marketing through Amazon in the U.S., UK, Australia, and other countries.
- ➢ Fast recognition of your work in your area of specialization.
- ➢ Quality design and affordable sales pricing. Using the latest technology, our books are produced efficiently, quickly and attractively.
- ➢ A global marketing plan, including electronic and web marketing and review mailing.
- ➢ Four Book Series: Deep Education; Deep Language Learning; Signs & Symbols in Education; Language Education Policy.

Deep Institute Online !

For updates and more resources
Visit the Deep Institute Website:
deepinstitute.org

To contact the Press
publisher@deepeducationpress.org

Visit our website
deepeducationpress.org

- Facebook group on Signs & Symbols in Education:
  https://www.facebook.com/groups/EducationalSemiotics/
- Twitter: http://twitter.com/SignsSymbols

Correspondence

Francois Victor Tochon, Department of Curriculum & Instruction, Teacher Education Building, UW-Madison, 225 North Mills street, Madison, Wisconsin 53706 USA.

Fax: (608) 263-9992. E-mail: ftochon@education.wisc.edu

140

www.ingramcontent.com/pod-product-compliance
Lightning Source LLC
Chambersburg PA
CBHW070945230426
43666CB00011B/2569